DID REALLY SIGN UP FOR THIS?!

#LEADERSHIPTRUTHS
on how to drive, thrive... and survive

GLAIN ROBERTS-MCCABE

Tellwell Talent
www.tellwell.ca

ISBN
978-1-77370-674-0 (Paperback)
978-1-77370-675-7 (eBook)

Dedication

This book is dedicated
to those who've entered
the leadership arena,
fallen down, got back
up and kept on trying to
get better. I salute you.

TABLE OF CONTENTS

#Know Yourself 36

#Manage Your Career 53

Section 2: Lead with Purpose   85

Section 3: Grow Your People   101

#Manage Yourself 102

#People: The Tricky Bits 118

Section 4: Deliver Results   143

#GetShitDone but Don't Burn Out 144

#That's a Wrap   163

#Keep Learning   165

Welcome to the Jungle!

"It is not the critic who counts; not the man who points out how the strong man stumbles, or where the doer of deeds could have done them better. **The credit belongs to the man who is actually in the arena**, whose face is marred by dust and sweat and blood; who strives valiantly; who errs, who comes short again and again, because there is no effort without error and shortcoming; but who does actually strive to do the deeds; who knows great enthusiasms, the great devotions; who spends himself in a worthy cause; who at the best knows in the end the triumph of high achievement, and who at the worst, if he fails, at least fails while daring greatly, so that his place shall never be with those cold and timid souls who neither know victory nor defeat."

- Theodore Roosevelt

I love this quote. It really nails what it means to be a leader. There are so many people who are quick to tell us, as leaders, what we're doing wrong, how we're screwing things up, how WE need to do and be better.

I always joke that my first leadership role was when I was just shy of my second birthday and the first of my three younger brothers arrived on the scene. They say that the oldest child is prone to leadership roles (aka being bossy) and, although I never really aspired to be the person in charge, I did always seem to find my way into leadership roles.

My first 'real' experience leading others was back in the early 1990s (a kinder, gentler time). I was tasked with leading teams of volunteers on various fundraising events. Managing people you don't pay and who technically don't really report to you is an excellent foundation for learning how to lead. Since that early experience, I've led teams in a variety of different profit and not-for-profit organizations. Along the way, I've thought several times to myself *'Did I REALLY sign up for this?!'* I even actively stepped out of leadership roles twice, thinking that maybe I wasn't cut out for them. But, like the proverbial moth to the flame, the desire to lead others and make a difference has always brought me back.

Learning to be a good leader, for me, is a lifelong journey that offers a variety of conflicting combinations: frustrating and fulfilling, terrifying and exhilarating, thankless and unbelievably rewarding. There are times when I feel like I've done things well and have really made an impact. There are other times (MANY other times) when I feel like I've really screwed things up.

That's leadership.

That's life.

This book for all of you who are out in the arena of leadership, working hard each and every day, trying to get better. This book is for anyone who ever felt like they were totally derailing on some days and King/Queen of the Universe on others. This book is for leaders who genuinely want to make an impact but sometimes don't know how to take the damn animation off their PowerPoint slides. It's for those who are driving forward, surviving setbacks and are intent on thriving in our careers.

This is for those of you who are really, really trying to do what's right for your teams, your companies and your families... but often put your own needs on a back burner along the way. This is for everyone who's ever messed up and lived to tell the tale.

The chapters that you'll find here have been curated from various RoundtableTalk blog posts written over the past decade. The ideas and lessons that I share come from years of observing, reflecting and analyzing leaders and their (and my own) leadership challenges.

This isn't a book on 'how to be a great leader'. I don't believe in silver bullets. My aim here is to help you find sources of inspiration when you need them, tools and ideas that you can put into action immediately, and the occasional kick in the pants, as required.

In an effort to put ten years of random thoughts into a cohesive whole, I've organized the posts into broad themes that follow our leadership model here at The Roundtable. For us, great leaders need to **be intentional**. This means:

- Know Yourself (aka It All Starts With You, Baby)
- Lead With Purpose
- Grow Your People
- Deliver Results

Dive into the topics that catch your eye and enjoy our random 'leadership truths' spread throughout the book.

Happy leading!

BE INTENTIONAL

(aka It All Starts with You, Baby)

Section 1

#GET AHEAD

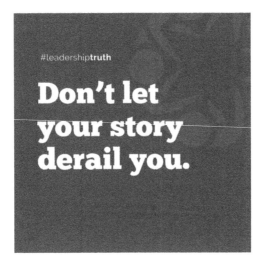

#leadership**truth**

Don't let your story derail you.

I have this tape continuously playing in my head that tells me that I'm not good enough. Most of us have a version of this tape. Our tapes get embedded in our brains from an early age usually as a result of parenting, school teachers or other influencers. On this tape are some of the stories we tell ourselves about our abilities and potential that do nothing but limit us and, sometimes, they actually work to derail our efforts. I have a story that I tell myself: that I'm an emotional eater, and I overeat when I get stressed. It consistently derails my attempts to eat healthily. I also have another story that I tell myself: that I'm not a very patient person (because, after all, my dad wasn't very patient). I often use this tape as an excuse when I've behaved in a way that I'm not particularly proud of. Getting rid of old tapes isn't easy but, with practiced reflection, you can slowly start to identify patterns and create a new dialog for yourself. Consistency and focus are key. I still don't think I'm as patient as I could be, but I'm leaps and bounds better than I used to be.

Job Hunters: Build Your Resilience like an Entrepreneur

One of the hardest things about self-employment is dealing with the never-ending, ongoing rollercoaster of highs and lows that come with building a business. Being able to manage the ride is something that I'm perpetually working on. One of the things I've learned about entrepreneurship is that it's exactly like job hunting. People ask me for tips to stay resilient as an entrepreneur, and I think the strategies I use are equally applicable for people who are job hunting.

I've had my own business now for just over ten years. From the outside, I get a lot of accolades for what I've achieved. What people don't see is what happens behind the curtain. Here's a taste:

- My three biggest clients all imploded over the span of three months, right after I'd expanded the business.
- My new hire quit after four months. I saw it coming, but refused to pay attention to the signs.
- I spent last week drowning in parts of the business that don't play to my strengths, making me wonder if getting a steady paycheque wouldn't be easier.
- My new client keeps moving back our project launch meetings, and money that I thought I could count on this month may not show up for another six months.

Get the picture?

So, how do I stay sane? Here are my tips:

Meditate. This has literally transformed my life. Instead of worrying about what *might* happen, I stay focused in the now and what *is* happening. Worrying – about money in particular – has a spectacular way of grinding your business (or job hunt) to a halt.

Be grateful. Man, what a privilege it is to live in Canada and do work like this. If I find myself throwing a pity party, I just think about people who would trade their challenges for mine in a nanosecond.

Energize yourself up. Smart people who love what they do give me energy. Learning gives me energy. Nature gives me energy. Speaking gives me energy. Knowing what gives you energy is key to building resilience.

Manage your week. Last week, for me, had way too many draining activities that involved accounting, taxes and administrative minutia. This week, I've got a better balance with client brainstorming, thinking time and public speaking. As much as possible, I try to balance my weeks with things that energize me vs. drain me. Know what gives you "juice" and try to build at least a few of those activities into your day to maintain your motivation.

Build your network. Entrepreneurs are generally pretty supportive. When I'm really feeling beaten up, I'll call one of my entrepreneurial friends who will quickly remind me that I've lived through these highs and lows before and will make it through to the other side. Make sure you galvanize your support system.

Many people say to me: "I could never do what you do." I fully disagree. Entrepreneurship isn't easy, but neither is looking for a new job. If you've ever persisted in finding a new position after being unemployed, believe me, you'd probably survive just fine as an entrepreneur.

Remember, it's all about building your resilience and playing the long game.

Net-leeching: How to Suck the Goodwill out of Your Network

At The Roundtable, we are flag-waving-champions on the importance of building and maintaining your personal and professional network. In work, your network will be one of the most crucial tools you'll ever "own". My friend Charles Brown, President of the Source, talks about the importance of having a small, tight network as a way to ensure job-option longevity. In my experience, meeting people and engaging them in your network is the easy part. The hard part is the maintenance. Recently, I was reminded of how NOT to maintain a network effectively and have coined a new phrase to describe it: net-leeching!

A few weeks ago, two of my clients and I received a 'networking' email from someone we all know peripherally who is currently looking for work. The response we all gave was pure annoyance. We essentially rolled our collective eyes and promptly deleted the request for support (admittedly after a slightly high school back and forth exchange behind the scenes about how annoying the request was in the first place). Why this harsh reaction, you ask? Well here's the story: this person had literally bled their network goodwill dry through a series of consistent miss-steps.

Here's how they went from a "networker" to a "net-leecher" and what you should avoid so that you don't get labelled a goodwill blood sucker:

No value-added... Every "stay in touch" email received from this individual contained updates on their career progress with no interesting information for the reader (other than hearing, once again, how fabulous this individual is).

No reciprocity... After the pitch ("keep me in mind for new roles"), the email ends with a bland "would love to hear what's new with you" which then gets zero response when you do send a follow-up (obviously leading one to question the sincerity of the sender).

No WIIFY... Tim Cork, author of *Tapping the Iceberg*, uses the term "net-giving" to describe how effective networking is about give and take. The key to building strong networks is to focus on how you can help the other person (vs. what they should be doing for you). Needless to say, on top of not really caring how the recipient is doing, our "net-leecher" never bothers to ask what they could do to help either.

TMI... Not that kind of "too much information", but hearing a regular annual or bi-annual update from someone who is gainfully employed asking to be kept in mind for other job opportunities actually has the opposite effect. Our network strength is based on the strength of our recommendations. Do you really want to recommend someone who always seems to have their eye out for another opportunity? Probably not.

By definition, a leech is someone who benefits from someone else's information, but doesn't offer anything in return. Don't be a net-leech. Your network requires a continuous investment of your time and attention. Just like in John F. Kennedy's historic speech, "ask not what your network can do for you, but what you can do for your network". When you really need the help, you'll want people to be anxious to reach out, not exchanging snarky emails behind your back and adding your name to the top of the list of people they DON'T want to help.

And, PS... If you meet with me while you're "unemployed" and looking for work and then neglect to keep in touch when you've landed something (especially if I've made the job introduction for you), please don't come knocking on my door again for another coffee next time you need a job. Just saying.

The #1 Question to Ask a Prospective Employer Before You Take the New Gig

As you go up the leadership ranks and build your successful track record, there's no doubt that – from time to time – some new opportunity will beckon or some new employer is going to come courting. Everyone knows that there's a degree of sunshine that gets blown up your backside during the interview dance, but in my experience, there's only one question you ever need to ask to know if the new gig is right for you.

Are you ready? (Insert drum roll here.)

"What is the tenure of senior people in this organization?"

That's it. That is truly the one question that is going to give you the "real deal" about what it's really like to work there.

When you hit your mid-career, I find there's a certain "been there, done that" mindset when it comes to compromising your values and putting in time under dysfunctional leadership. If you're heading into a role that puts you in the direct report zone of the company President or one key level below, this question is the one to ask to make sure that the leadership of the company fits with where you want to put your talents.

If the answer comes back that the tenure of senior level employees is less than two years, call that a big, fat, red flag (call it a reason to run if the person is an entrepreneur). Dig deeper and find out why people have left. If the reasons sound fishy, they probably are and you need to take a close look at the leadership style of "el Presidente". It's probably bordering on abusive. Most smart people at senior levels don't stick around for long or put up with that type of behaviour, so a revolving door is a clear sign that something is amiss.

If the tenure is really, really long then find out why. Is the CEO a superstar or is he/she just surrounded by a bunch of yes people? If you're an ambitious "mix it up" type of person, you may not fit in a conservative leadership culture and may need to take a pass. I've seen many talented people fail because their leadership style didn't fit with the dominant culture created by the CEO and his/her top team.

CEOs cast a long shadow on their organizations. In my experience, one of the best ways to find out whether it's one that you want to stand under is to find out more about your peer group and whether the fit is going to be right. Revolving door leaders aren't right for high performers like you.

Chase the Dream, Not the Paper

I once had the opportunity to hear Zappos' head happiness spreader, Tony Hsieh, talk about his team's winning formula for business success. After sitting through a few career and coaching discussions involving money, titles and career satisfaction, I kept coming back to a quote Hsieh used in his talk: **"Chase the dream, not the paper."**

Hsieh credited P. Diddy with this little gem, which was lifted from a (likely) Oscar-winning moment in the movie *Notorious* about the east coast rapper Notorious B.I.G. In Hsieh's case, Zappos' focus is on making their customers happy and not making the company profitable (the thinking being that happy customers lead to a happy bottom line).

From my perspective, chasing the dream and not the paper is applicable whether you're running a business or managing your career. In my experience, most of the people I know who love their jobs (i.e. they're really passionate about what they do) make lots of money and (even if they have high pressure jobs) are pretty stress-free. On the flip side, people I know who don't love their jobs but make lots of money seem to spend a lot of time throwing around words like "golden handcuffs" and seem to be perpetually stressed.

When it comes to long-term career happiness, money and titles wear off pretty quickly. Twenty, thirty or forty years is a really long time to be doing something that makes you miserable, don't you think? For leaders, I think this is even more crucial. How can you inspire others if your heart isn't into what you're doing? And, really, isn't inspiring others one of the greatest opportunities that the choice of leadership presents?

So, the homework assignment for all of you "handcuffed" big title, big salary types out there is this: go and buy Gary Vaynerchuk's book *Crush It* and figure out what's holding you back from chasing your dream.

Ramp Your Career Through Volunteering

One of the most underutilized ways to advance your career is to consider volunteering on Boards. By joining a Board, you are expanding your network of influencers and getting an opportunity to demonstrate your skills in real-time. But before you run off and start putting your name forward to every not-for-profit or for-profit Board opening, here are some tips to make sure you're ready:

Be sure you love it. Volunteering on a Board can be flattering and may help build lots of career connections, but if you don't love the cause, it may turn into more of a grind than you'd like.

Hone two crucial skills. To participate at the Board level, in addition to the expertise you're bringing to the table, you'll need a basic understanding of financial statements and some sense of board governance. It's important to know your role and responsibilities.

Do your due diligence. Before jumping in, make sure the fit is right for you. Take a close look at the dynamics of the Board, the decision-making process, the stage of the organization's life cycle (newer organizations will be far more hands-on than more established ones), and its overall culture. Board leadership is very different than organizational leadership, so make sure the group you're joining is one you can work with.

Check out the Chairperson. The Board Chairperson is a pivotal role. Get to know that individual and their leadership style before committing to the group. If you fear that your Chair has Machiavellian tendencies, step down quickly and, if you're brave enough, do what you can to blow the whistle on their behaviour.

Flex your collaborative muscle. Boards are a collective leadership group with each member holding equal voting rights. Unlike corporate leadership, where you may get away with a "my way or the highway" approach, Board work will require you to flex your consensus-building and collaborative muscles. It's a great place to learn leadership via informal influence.

It's who you know. Board members are given a great deal of responsibility and therefore, members want to feel comfortable and trust those who are sitting around the table with them. Most Board referrals come from existing relationships and word-of-mouth referrals.

Work your way up. If you don't have any existing Board member friends and would like to make your way onto a Board, start with a committee. This will allow others to see you in action and help you become the "known entity" you need to be to get considered for a Board post.

Education is advised. Whether you look at groups like BoardMatch, ICD or other local organizations, additional training will help you get ready for your Board responsibilities. It won't guarantee you a post on a Board, but it will help you know what you're doing when you get to the table.

Volunteering is a wonderful way to genuinely give back, share your expertise and continue to challenge yourself. You'll build incredible relationships and have the opportunity to truly make a difference to the organization and the people you're supporting.

Lessons Learned in the Pursuit of Career Happiness

I spent the better part of my 30s being afraid to do what I really wanted to do with my life, which was to run my own business. It wasn't that I wasn't good at being an employee. I think I was a pretty textbook high performer. I got promoted quickly, got tagged for succession roles and typically had a good relationship with my bosses. Despite all this, I had a hard time with authority and was continuously concocting business ideas. But I was afraid. Afraid to leave the security of a paycheque, and afraid to take the leap. Thanks to my husband, after close to seven years of thinking about it, I finally did it. And since that first leap in January 2007, this is what I've learned about overcoming your fears and pursuing your passions:

You can't run away from your calling. If you're meant to be doing something, the "universe" is going to push you to do it. In my case, I ended up finding myself in an abusive employment relationship where the fear of losing my sanity trumped my fear of quitting my job. If you ignore the universe it just starts beating you with a bigger stick.

You always have a choice. When I talk to other people who are unhappy doing what they're doing, they'll often blame their financial responsibilities: mortgages, private schools, car payments, etc. Here's the thing: when I quit my job, I was the breadwinner and my husband was at home with our three year-old daughter. We had no family support and a $300,000 mortgage. That first year was financial hell and was really hard on my marriage. I would never recommend it to anyone. My husband kept saying: "We're going to lose the house." We did end up selling and moving to another one in a less desirable neighbourhood. And guess what? It was the best thing we ever did.

We have fantastic neighbours. The mortgage (and every other bill) could be covered by my husband's income and this financial relief allowed me to fully focus on my business. After that first year of hell, it's been a steady upward climb. Which leads me to my next point…

When you do what you really love, the money does take care of itself. I worry about money quite a bit. It's probably because I ran away from home at 17 and have supported myself ever since. I have a high need for independence, which money gives you. I didn't start my business as a way to make money – in fact, this is probably the worst field for anyone with major "get rich quick" desires. I just truly felt like I could contribute something that would help other ambitious leaders. There have been many times over the past years of self-employment that I have worried about money and every time something has come through when I've needed it. I can't explain it. It just happens. But let's be clear…

Following your passion is the hardest work you'll ever do. When I'm having a bad day at work, my husband will say: "You're doing what you love. You're supposed to be in a perpetual state of bliss." It's a good thing I love him and appreciate his sense of humour. Even when you're on your life's path, there are going to be days when it's not easy. And doing what you love doesn't mean that you're not going to need to work hard. Really hard. But it really is a different kind of hard work. Today, I have more responsibility than I ever had in my previous jobs (when other people's paycheques are on your back, it's intense) but I'm far less stressed out today than I ever was when I was on someone else's payroll.

Don't listen to so-called experts. When you are about to embark on something big, something that scares you and excites you at the same time, fear will begin to raise its ugly head. It may come in the form of words from family and friends or it may be through other means. For me, it was those stupid online tests that tell you whether you should be an entrepreneur. (Apparently, because my parents weren't entrepreneurs, I'm not really cut out to be one, either.) When you're breathing down the neck of your life's passion, it is easy to let fear derail your plans and provide you with a safety net to justify quitting. Don't. What's on the other side of fear is amazing. But remember this…

Fear is a tenacious little bastard. As humans, we are continuously growing and evolving. Unfortunately, our fears can evolve with us along the way. What used to scare me in my early years as a business owner no longer scares me, but other fears are raising their head even as I type this. The thing that I have learned is that once you face down your fear the first time, it gets easier to face it down subsequently. Your track record of success will build the confidence you need to keep going and growing.

Whatever your calling is—to transition to a new job or industry, to take that promotion you don't feel you're ready for, to move to the hills and sell pottery—please don't let fear strangle your dreams. Too many people are living their lives trapped in careers counting down the days to retirement. This world needs your talents. Don't suffocate these talents with misplaced fears and self-limiting beliefs. The journey to find your purpose may not be an easy one, but I promise you, it's worth the effort.

Jerks, Narcissists and Psychopaths, Oh My. When Working for a Lousy Leader Might Pay Off.

Ah, to have the ability to click your heels together and transport yourself away from a bad boss! They seem to be everywhere these days, but after watching Anna Wintour of Vogue in the fascinating movie *The September Issue*, I began to wonder if there were any career benefits to working for an abusive boss.

The September Issue chronicles the development and release of the September issue of Vogue (the biggest and most important issue of the fashion year). The documentary film crew follow Vogue's editor-in-chief, the legendary drag-on-lady Anna Wintour, and her chief creative director Grace Coddington as they stalk each other through to the finished product.

This is yet another fascinating view at leadership in action and starkly contrasts the styles of the two icons, Wintour and Coddington.

Coddington is approachable, authentic and kind. Frankly, this woman looks like someone who might be working as a Walmart greeter as opposed to being the top creative director at Vogue! Despite her obvious talent (and therefore potential for hauling around a big ego), she is shown making sure that the catering crew save a piece of strawberry tart for one of her models, helping a junior staffer navigate "Ms. Wintour" and seeing that a man's tummy isn't airbrushed out of a final studio shot. People seem to enjoy working with and for her, and she gets great results.

Wintour, on the other hand, lives up to her "Devil Wears Prada"-inspired reputation, with icy remarks to employees that would make the most secure person question their own competence (check out the last scene in the official trailer). It's hilarious to watch her try and maintain a façade of control when bad news is presented to her. You get the distinct impression that, if the cameras hadn't been rolling, a major hissy fit would have occurred! And, there's a scene between Wintour and Coddington as they wait in a lobby for an elevator which is absolutely painful to watch. The tension between the two is palpable.

Certainly Wintour has been a star performer for *Vogue* and carries major weight in the world of fashion. But is all this nastiness really necessary and why do people as talented as Grace Coddington continue to work for her?

The answer may be that when someone is truly exceptional at what they do (i.e. they really are a genius), the payoff in what you can learn from them allows you to overlook their lousy leadership behaviour. Working for a nasty twit probably wouldn't hold the same appeal.

If you can stomach it for a year or two, the amount you can learn from a true (evil) genius about their area of expertise could be worth more than 10 MBAs stacked end-to-end. Just please don't repeat the lousy leadership part of the equation when you emerge from your prison-like employment. After all, workplaces could, in my humble opinion, use more Grace Coddington-type leaders than the Anna Wintour-type leaders.

Career Management for the Easily Distracted

What are you going to be when you grow up? Have you figured that out yet? Feeling pressure that you don't have a "career plan"? Well, don't worry: you're not alone. I've had the chance to interview many senior leaders over the years and most don't have a clue how they ended up where they are today.

Peter Aceto, the former CEO of Tangerine Bank, laughed when I asked him if he'd always known he was going to be a bank CEO and said: *"Was I supposed to have a plan?"* I have encountered people in my career who do have plans, but they seem to be very few and far between... and I'm not sure that they're particularly happy. If you struggle with setting career goals, a technique that you might want to try is the 3-year vivid vision technique used by many entrepreneurs.

Think about your retirement and ask yourself these questions (assuming you could be doing anything you want):

1. **How will I be spending my time in the final years leading up to my retirement?**

   Write it down. What will you be doing? How will you be spending your days? What activities, if you could do anything at all, would you be doing? What type of business are you working in? What type of role do you have?

   Don't censor yourself. Don't limit your thinking. If you would be guiding tourists down the Amazon, write it down. If you see yourself running a surf shack on a beach, write it down. Don't worry how you'll get there.

2. **What actions can I take over the next 12 to 18 months that will move me closer to achieving this vision?**

Once you've done that, break those activities down into what you will accomplish in the next 30 to 90 days.

3. **What's the one thing I can do each week to move my vision forward?**

At the end of the year, you'll have done 52 things that put you closer to your career vision. How cool is that?

I've noticed that many people say that they want to shift careers or change jobs or do something different but get immediately overwhelmed with what it's going to take to make that career shift happen (five years to get another degree part–time!). As I get older, I realize just how quickly five years can fly by.

As the old saying goes: "The best time to plant an oak tree was 10 years ago; the second-best time is today." Think about the small, incremental changes you can make to move your plan forward. You can do it.

Tithe Your Development

The act of tithing—giving 10% of your earnings to church, charity or 'taxes'—is a practice that goes back to Ancient Times. David Chilton made millions by introducing a modern-day twist on tithing through his book *The Wealthy Barber*. Chilton challenged people to 'pay themselves first' by putting aside 10% of their income into savings. Well, I've got a new challenge on tithing for anyone who's in the knowledge economy: take 10% of your income and invest it into professional development. Here's why:

The world is accelerating. I have a diploma in creative advertising that I earned in 1989 which is, today, pretty much useless. If I'd continued in that career path (world domination as a creative director at an ad agency), I'd be toast if I wasn't continually upping my knowledge on the latest consumer trends and marketing tools. The fact that you took a semester program in your MBA on leadership isn't going to make you a great leader. Forget it. I've been doing this for over 25 years and I'm still learning.

Your brand has a limited shelf life. Thanks to this frenetic pace of change, what made you a superstar last year in your role may not be what the company is going to be looking for next year. You need to keep evolving, not just in terms of your skills but also your behaviours. In the age of collaboration, it's all about Emotional Intelligence (EQ) baby.

You change. Simple. Who you are today is different than who you were 10 years ago. And if not, then you're on a quick path to personal atrophy. For leaders, in particular, your strength will always, always, always lie in the degree of self-insight you have. If you're not investing in continually exploring your mindsets, beliefs and motivations, then you are walking around with some MASSIVE blind spots that have the potential to derail you.

Personal development is not a one-shot thing. Sure, completing college or university or even high school is important. Education is important. But it doesn't stop when you walk across the stage in that cap and gown. We invest tens of thousands of dollars into our degrees and diplomas, but when it comes to hiring a coach or taking a course, we shudder. Education isn't an expense, it's an investment. Reframe your thinking.

Many people are fortunate enough to work for companies that will cover development programs, but if you're not one of the "lucky" ones, then tithing 10% of your income for personal development is a must. Think about it: if you earn $100,000, you can do some KICK ASS programs for $10,000. You don't even need to spend nearly that much!

I have invested tens of thousands of dollars on myself over the years from my own pocket. From coaches that charged $3,000 a month to courses that cost $10,000, I can honestly say I have NEVER, EVER, EVER regretted any decision I made, because it was MY decision (which is different than when your company sends you on some awful training program that you don't need). I do things that I'm interested in and that keep me sharp. For the last four years, I've taken a weekly meditation class. Right now, I'm doing a certificate in Team and Group Coaching. Add up the number of lattes you buy in a year, I bet you can afford a pretty wicked development experience from that cost alone!

So, to keep your edge, keep investing in yourself. Don't you think you're worth it? I do.

#KNOW YOURSELF

My Dad had a saying: Never believe so-called "experts". His point being that most of the time, when people advised him to do things with a degree of "authority", their ideas were usually no better than his own. I've learned that we often underestimate our expertise and look to others for guidance. Usually, we know exactly what we need to do, we just need to trust ourselves to do it. What expertise of your own are you currently underestimating?

Core Values: Not Just for Warm, Fuzzy Life Coaches

Through my 20s, I was the poster girl for the GenX job jumper. It wasn't until my early 30s when, tired of jumping, I completed a career management coaching program and did an exercise to uncover my "values". My friend John, who debriefed the results, told me something that hit a deep chord and explained so many reasons as to why I was struggling in my then-role:

"You're going to need a very high degree of autonomy to be happy in the long run."

Throughout my career, my path had looked something like this (give or take a few months):

Year 1: Join company, learn as much as possible, listen to and respect my boss, somehow become a star employee.

Year 2: Start wishing that my boss would leave me the hell alone now that I know more about the job than s/he does. Become an employee who delivers results but argues with the boss too much.

Year 3: Leave before getting fired for killing said boss. *(Just kidding… usually by year 3 I was bored. If I hadn't been given more things to send me out of my comfort zone, and was not wanting to become a pain in the neck to my boss, I moved on.)*

Once I understood that one of my values was an incredibly high need for autonomy, independence and flexibility, I could recognize how having a boss of any kind was making me crazy. Don't get me wrong, I had some GREAT bosses and have learned a ton from them, but even the best boss was too much for someone like me who needed to run their own show.

Fast forward six years after that fateful conversation about my values with John, and I found myself swinging from the corporate ledge into the world of self-employment.

What I've learned about values is that they're not just "fluffy" words that life coaches use. They drive our personal decisions and life choices – whether we realize it or not.

Once you get clear on what really matters, decision-making becomes so much easier, as does identifying why things at work may be rubbing you the wrong way. Take some time to explore your values. I guarantee you won't regret it.

Are Those REALLY Your Strengths?

In 1999, I read Marcus Buckingham and Curt Coffman's ground-breaking book *First Break All the Rules: What Great Managers Do Differently*. It's all about strengths-based leadership and it changed how I thought of my own strengths and how I thought about my role as a manager of others. It changed how I thought of my own strengths and how I thought about my role as a manager of others. I jumped onto the strengths bandwagon hard. I began to tirelessly focus on my own and endeavoured to have "strengths-based" discussions with my direct reports. I even worked in a consulting firm that embraced the "work to your strengths" philosophy and put a big emphasis on not fitting a "square peg into a round hole" and making sure we were getting the right people into the "right seat on the bus".

Several years later, I heard Buckingham speak about strengths and had the horrific realization that I had only been partially correct in my view of what a "strength" really was. I had interpreted that my strengths were partly what I enjoyed doing and was good at, but also what other people told me I was good at and what I got rewarded for (performance). And here lies the problem.

What Buckingham pointed out is that when you're using your true "strengths", you feel energized and engaged, not exhausted and depleted. True strengths have less to do with your performance ability and more to do with the personal "juice" you get out of the experience. In many cases, especially as you get more "seasoned" in leadership, you learn how to manage your weaknesses, and can even get quite skilled at things that you don't particularly enjoy doing. For example, as a leader, I love the "big ideas" and hate having to wade around in the details of execution. That being said, if you saw me in action you would think that I'm actually very good with details, which is true… just don't make me do that type of work all the time!

Buckingham suggests that we should call these things that we're good at, but that we don't enjoy, anything BUT strengths. Strengths are things you love to do.

To help you begin to catalog the things that are your strengths, he suggested you try this exercise for a week:

Keep a diary and list all the activities that you do throughout the day. Jot them down as you do them (don't try and reflect back at the end of the day or the week do it in real time). Notice how you FELT when you were doing the activity (e.g.: energized, frustrated, engaged, tired, etc.). Catalog your activities under two columns: loved or loathed.

Then, at the end of the week, write a strengths statement and a weakness statement.

The key to the exercise is to make sure it is an activity that YOU are doing (e.g.: "I feel strong when I'm solving complicated problems with smart people"), not something that is being done by someone else to you (e.g.: "I feel strong when I receive recognition from my boss").

Over the course of our careers, we will have many well-intentioned managers tell us what our strengths are. And, if we're not careful, we can have a very successful career doing things we loathe, but that we're good at. Don't let your manager determine your career path by pushing you into jobs or experiences that you're good at but don't enjoy. Keep paying attention to those things that give you "juice". Keep sharing those things with your manager so that you can move into a role where you can do what you are great at AND what you are energized by.

Brand Statements: What's the Point?

In 1998, Tom Peters wrote for *Fast Company* what I think of as the seminal article on personal branding. In it, Peters challenged readers to think of themselves in marketing terms as a sellable "brand" that needed to be proactively cultivated. Read it now and it could have been written yesterday, not decades ago. Since then, an entire industry has evolved around people helping you "build your brand" by creating personal brand statements. The question I often get asked is: "Now that I've got the brand statement, what am I supposed to do with it?"

I've got some ideas, but first, let's be clear on what a good brand statement is and what it isn't. Saying "I'm a strategic thinker adept at rallying teams and using my analytical skills to solve problems" is not a good brand statement. Any middle manager could say the same thing. The point (in my opinion) of a brand statement is to help you stand out from the crowd, to showcase what makes you unique. How are you a linchpin?

In our Roundtable programs, we encourage individuals to write their brand statements "Twitter-style", that is, in short, illustrative bursts: "I'm a Talent Magnet. Champion of Authenticity. Solutions Sherlock. Pragmatic Optimist. Curator of Conversations."

Now, depending on the context, when asked to describe who you are, you may not deliver this message in quite as punchy a fashion. But that's not the point. The point is that these qualities are things that anchor you and how you do what you do uniquely. So, here's how you can use your brand statement:

1. **To clarify your career goals.** Post your brand statement somewhere you can see it, or keep a copy in your wallet to refer to when you're evaluating next career moves. Refer to it to evaluate if the opportunities you're exploring are lining up with the brand you want to build and reinforce for yourself.

2. **To attract attention.** LinkedIn is becoming the go-to source for recruiters and HR executives looking for fresh talent. A strong brand statement or brand phrases can be used in place of your current title and in your "background" paragraph to push you up the search rankings.

3. **To engage your team.** Share who you are and what you stand for, and encourage your team to do the same. Having team members develop their own brand statements increases opportunities for you to further coach and mentor them towards meaningful career paths.

4. **To stand out.** Many resumes open with the *yawn* career objective statement. Replace the career objective with your brand statement and stand out from the sea of sameness.

Those are just a few ways you can use a brand statement. For more information on how to build your brand statement, check out the work of William Arruda, who is an absolute expert in this field by visiting his website at http://williamarruda.com/.

Authenticity: How Real Can You Really Be?

"Be yourself, everyone else is taken," said Ralph Waldo Emerson. But what if being yourself is a career limiting move? How much of yourself is smart to show at work? In 2012, we had an executive panel on this very topic and leaders Simon Jennings (then President of Gesca Media Sales), Pam Laycock (then SVP of Corporate Strategy and Development, Torstar Corporation) and Rosemarie McClean (SVP, Members Services, Ontario Teachers' Pension Plan) joined our podium to share their ideas and perspectives on this hot topic. Here are some of their thoughts:

What is authenticity exactly?

- Staying true to what you believe in and acting in accordance with your beliefs.

- Taking on new challenges, but still being true to yourself. You can't chameleon yourself to an environment if you don't feel comfortable in your own skin.

- Following your own best instincts. When you are a young leader, you get guidance, which might not always be right. If something doesn't feel right to you… don't do it.

- Being consistent.

How can you tell if someone is being inauthentic? And why is it such a big deal?

- When you don't act authentically, you come across as being phony. People won't know if they can truly trust you, and nobody wants to follow a leader they can't trust. Leaders are always being watched, so your actions need to align with your words.

- You cannot get 100% out of someone who is being inauthentic. You always feel that there's something they're holding back.

But what about politics? Don't we need to sometimes "act" a certain way to get ahead?

- Politics aren't always negative. They are often needed to get things done. As a leader, you do have to understand how to play the game in order to get to the finish line.

- The key is to not compromise who you are and to make sure that the politics are for the greater good vs. advancing your own personal agenda.

Authenticity starts with you.

- As an executive, you can influence culture. In fact, it is your responsibility to shape culture. Leaders have to think how their behaviours will impact employees and model the way.

- Leaders have the responsibility to drive authenticity and to call out colleagues who aren't walking the talk. This takes courage!

- Know your own strengths and what type of corporate culture will allow you to be successful. Pay attention to the culture created by the senior leadership team. Trying to change a corporate culture by yourself will be a futile exercise, so make sure the fit really is there. Don't get deluded by your own abilities.

- Balance your outside and inside persona, otherwise you'll come across as fake.

- People are always watching, looking for consistency and openness.

- You cannot control your environment; you can only control your impact.

From my perspective, if you find yourself not able to be yourself at work, it's probably because it's not the right cultural fit for you. We all need to adapt certain aspects of our behaviours to work/play well with others. However, if you feel like you have to put on a completely different persona to make it through the workday, odds are, it simply isn't the place for you. Find something that's better aligned to your values and beliefs so that you can bring more of yourself to work each day.

Navigating Leadership's Toughest Role: the Middle!

I don't care what any C-level executive says, it's not just lonely at the top; it's also lonely in the middle on the way to the top! And today, the people who have the toughest job in any organization, in my book, are the mid-level leaders. If you're a Senior Manager, Director or two or more level down VP, hats off to you my friends: you are some of the bravest people in leadership out there.

Here are some tips on how to thrive in leadership's toughest gig:

It's all about self-insight. Get a 360 assessment (feedback from boss, peers and direct reports) done and act on it. Actively seek ways to get perspective on your leadership so that you're aware of your blind spots. The higher you get, the more important it is to know where your strengths and opportunities lie.

Manage your own career. Don't expect the organization to do it for you. Be proactive about developing yourself and managing your network. Your career is an investment – when things don't go right, you want to be armed with resources and a network to help you get back on track.

Stand out by getting curious. Be proactive about learning about other parts of the business. Ask questions. Get to know how your area impacts others. Not only will you be seen as a "go-getter", you'll also be building your strategy muscle and be better able to position yourself as someone capable of taking on bigger scope.

Follow your strengths, not the status. Try not to be seduced by titles or money. Look for opportunities that allow you to continually hone what you're good at. Pay attention to your strengths. If you find yourself in a role that isn't working for you, address it quickly.

Be the leader in your peer group. Connect with your peers regularly. Actively seek ways to take the reins around shared issues. When you are seen as the natural leader of your peer group, chances are you'll be seen as the natural choice for promotion (and will have the goodwill of your former peers to back you).

Tune in to the top. Know the priorities of your boss' boss. What are the things that keep them awake at night? Understanding these drivers will make your boss look good and will help you prioritize your day-to-day activities.

Seek support. Find a mentor, internal or external, such as joining a peer group or working with a coach. Most importantly, look for a boss who is supportive and whose values you align with. (And if your boss really stinks, try to see if you can make it work, but if not, move on. They'll likely be an obstacle for your career.)

Get mindful. Leadership at all levels can be lonely and those in the middle are typically under the most pressure. Make sure you're looking after yourself as you navigate this demanding space.

Motivation, Motivation, Wherefore Art Thou, Motivation?

Ever had one of those days where you just can't seem to get motivated to get anything done, despite the fact that your to-do list is about a thousand miles long? That's my day today in a nutshell. My Productivity Planner is staring me down and I'm actually wishing today that I was on somebody else's payroll so that I could feel less guilt about "slacking off". And then it hit me: I'm being a slave to my to-do list and haven't been paying attention to my energy level!!! Damn… I hate it when that happens.

You see, being self-employed is a bit of a double-edged sword. Sure, you have lots of freedom, but you also feel lots of guilt if you don't use your time effectively. Especially when you have other people on your payroll and you have a mountain of things to do.

Today, two clients cancelled on me, so I found myself with a large amount of free time. But I couldn't get motivated to do anything with it. So, I watched the trailer for the movie *Friends* (couldn't follow it), watched Alec Baldwin's latest stint on *Saturday Night Live*, organized my email in-basket (aka reacted to other people's agendas) and avoided some of the less pleasant things I have to get off my plate (budgeting, legal stuff and prospecting, blech).

And the guilt of all these shenanigans was setting in good and heavy. "I should be using this time more productively! I have clients to reach out to! Sales to close! People to connect with! Work, work, work, work, work!" The more I nagged myself, the less motivated I started to get. I actually felt myself getting bummed out.

And then I thought: "Fuck. That. Shit." It's time for a kick in the pants, but rather than powering through my to-do list, I decided to do something fun. I made a Facebook live post of our #12DaysofBizRAK campaign. #12DaysofBizRAK is 12 days of business Random Acts of Kindness for those of you who may not be aware. Then I wrote this post. And I realized that to get yourself out of a funk, you sometimes need to re-energize yourself with things that you actually like to do.

So, now that I'm feeling more plugged in, I'm going to get back to my prospecting.

Next time you're in a motivational funk, ignore your to-do list and do something that makes you happy instead. It might just give you the energy you need to do the stuff that's less interesting.

The Myth of the 'Perfect' Leader

Sometimes, when I give leadership talks, people will come up to me afterwards and tell me that they really appreciated my candour in talking about my shortcomings. I guess they think that because I am a leadership coach, I must be a perfect leader all the time (or at least pretend to be one when I'm getting paid to talk about leadership). I am far from perfect. But, I do try to be better. Some days I think I do pretty well; other days, not so much. Here's something that happened to me last week that I preach others not to do. See if you can relate.

On Thanksgiving Sunday, I started coming down with a cold. It hit me hard on Monday. I stayed in bed all day, then ended up working at home on Tuesday. By Wednesday, I was only slightly better but had a client session that I felt I couldn't cancel. So, I loaded up on drugs and headed off. I worked from home for the remainder of the week. By Friday, I still wasn't well. I hadn't fully committed to being off sick. Instead I was "lightly working", which meant that I wasn't sleeping well because I kept thinking about the things I needed to catch up on the next day.

Let me pause here and say that I know better than this. I teach sessions with our members on the importance of recovery, of how taking downtime is critical to both your physical and mental well-being.

Back to Friday. While on a Skype call with my colleagues, I declared that I was taking the afternoon off. I needed to "rest and rejuvenate" because obviously, working while sick wasn't helping me get any better.

I decided to get some fresh air and took my dog for a walk to the park. While she was off romping with her friends, I casually scrolled through emails and read an article that one of my colleagues had sent me. I shot off a quick response saying that I thought it was great. Realizing in the moment that I wasn't exactly role modelling positive behaviour (after all, I'd just finished saying that I was taking the afternoon off), I hastily added: "For the record, I'm writing this from the dog park." I received this wise response from my colleague:

> "Ummm… It doesn't matter if you are physically at the dog park if you are not "present" with her (and yourself).
>
> Your mind needs a rest as much as your body. Your brain needs to get back to a state of "coherence" because when it's not, it causes "disease" in your body.
>
> Not sure if you've yet seen a doctor? Although I'm not one, I'm going to go out on a limb and prescribe a remedy for you.
>
> Here it is:
>
> Put the phone away.
>
> Close your eyes.
>
> Take a few deep breaths.
>
> Let Go.
>
> Do it again.
>
> Take another deep breath.
>
> This time – really let go.
>
> Enjoy the sun on your face.
>
> Take in the moment.
>
> Soak up the beauty of the fall colours.
>
> Laugh at Bella.
>
> Laugh at yourself.

And know that you are blessed.

Be well." ☺

It's always good to work with people who aren't afraid to call you on your bullshit. I did turn off my phone for the rest of the afternoon and went to a walk-in clinic to get antibiotics.

I don't have to be a superhero at work, and neither do you. Take care of yourself so that you can take care of others. And no one is a perfect leader. The best we can do is learn from our mistakes and try a little better next time.

#MANAGE YOUR CAREER

When was the last time you developed yourself at work? Too busy, you say? Big targets to meet? In today's 24/7 world, where change is relentless, leaders who don't prioritize their self-development are at high risk of being left behind. In my observation, an advanced degree depreciates faster than the new car you just drove off the lot. Continuous learning isn't a "nice to-do", it's a necessity in this volatile, uncertain, complex and ambiguous "VUCA" world. So be strategic about your career and be sure to prioritize learning as a "must do" to keep yourself ahead of the trend and marketable.

Are Metaphors Killing Your Career?

I spend most of my time working with very ambitious, highly productive people who sit squarely in middle management. Middle management is a tricky area of the organizational chart to navigate. The biggest issue (as I see it) is that what got you to middle management often won't get you to the next level, and senior leaders, for the most part, are really lousy at telling you where you're falling short so that you can leap that hurdle.

The reality of the middle is that the things that got you to that point – your ability to get shit done – are now simply table stakes. The things that are going to get you ahead now are in the realm of "how you get shit done". And, that "how" feedback can come in very unclear and confusing ways. See if any of these statements sound familiar:

"We need you to step up and think 'bigger picture'."

"We need you to 'break something' and show us how you put it back together."

"You need to operate at the 50,000-foot view now, but know when to drop into the weeds."

"Don't forget, leadership casts a long shadow."

"Know when to throw a smack down."

"We need you to lead from the front."

I could go on. When delivering constructive feedback, many managers overplay storytelling and inadvertently become masters of confusion. Buried in the meaning of each of the statements above is a specific behaviour that you're either not demonstrating at all or demonstrating far too much. With statements this vague, you're at risk of continuously falling short of these new (unarticulated) expectations.

So, here's how you can take your career management back into your own hands. If your boss is hitting you with some vague metaphor around how they need you to change your leadership, thank them for the feedback and ask them this question: What's **one thing** that you could **start doing** that would demonstrate more of the behaviour they are looking for?

There, that's it. By asking for a specific action, your boss should be able to give you something more concrete. It's critical to note that the emphasis here is on the "start doing" aspect. It's easier to start a new habit or behaviour than stop an old one. For example, your boss says: "Don't be late for meetings." Just flip it around and make the action: "Start being 5 minutes early for meetings." Your boss may get on a roll and give you more than one thing. That's great. The more you have, the more you'll understand what they're looking for from you.

If you still don't feel like you fully understand your boss, paraphrase back what you think they said so that they can further elaborate if they need to. "So, if I hear you correctly, you would like me to be more assertive in meetings when things are going to affect my area by pushing back on Bob, versus accommodating him so frequently?" If you're off base, your boss will clarify it for you further.

Once you've got some specifics to work with, put them into action and follow-up with your boss on a monthly basis to see if s/he is seeing some progress. This may sound ridiculous, but it's important that you start getting your boss to look for the new behaviour vs. focusing on the old behaviours.

Don't let vague metaphors about performance derail your career. Make sure you understand what is required of you in your role in order to get positioned for all the opportunities you deserve.

Help! I've Been Pigeonholed

When my daughter was heading into grade 4, we tried to convince her to switch to a school closer to our home (she was still attending school in our former neighbourhood). My selling point was that she could reinvent herself at a new school. Sadly, she's pretty happy with her "rep" at her current school, so that pitch fell flat.

But there is a lot of truth to the fact that, when you switch to a new job, you leave behind any baggage from your previous employer that may be dogging you. If you're feeling like you're getting trapped in a pigeon-hole at work, here's a process to help you bust out of it courtesy of Marshall Goldsmith. The process is called FeedForward and it goes like this:

First, define the part of your personal brand that you want to change. You need to clearly label the behaviour that has created the reputation you want to shift. Here are some common "pigeon-holes" I see people getting stuck in:

- Too tactical, not strategic enough
- Not a good listener
- Too hotheaded
- Indecisive
- Overly emotional
- Too empathetic
- Nice guy who doesn't drive results

You probably get the picture. Once you've identified the behaviour, follow these steps:

1. **Identify people whose perception of your behaviour needs to change.** This is key. You need to start proactively getting people to see you in a different light.

2. **Set up one-on-one meetings with each person and explain how you want to work on this behaviour.** Ask them for some specific suggestions on what you can do differently to demonstrate what they're looking for. It might look like this:

"Hi Bob. I've realized that I'm a bit of a hothead at the office. This is something I'd really like to change. What is your best suggestion for me on how I can demonstrate keeping my cool?"

3. **Listen to their ideas.** Write them down and thank them for their input. Don't argue or debate them!

4. **Repeat this process until you've met with each stakeholder.** Congratulations! Now you have an action list of things you need to start saying and doing that will demonstrate the new behaviour you want to be known for (thus minimizing the derailing behaviour you want to shake). Note: your list of actions should be small and manageable. Pick one to two things to start doing purposefully and immediately.

5. **Put your plan into action at every opportunity.** Think about specific situations where you can demonstrate your new behaviours. Check in with your stakeholders to get their feedback about how you're doing and to make sure you're focusing on the right things.

6. **Continue with your plan until these new behaviours are no longer "new" but simply feel like part of your overall leadership repertoire.** Check in with stakeholders to see how your new brand is evolving.

The challenge for anyone who's been with a company for any length of time is that we can become labeled in ways that may or may not be accurate. By enlisting others to support your development efforts, you'll be changing their perception without having to change jobs.

The Pigeonhole Part II

We've all got a "brand". If I were to walk into any of your organizations and ask your peers, direct reports or boss to describe you to me, I'd get some various perspectives. But there would also be some common ground. Within a few minutes, I would know what your best traits and qualities are and what your most annoying, irritating or least helpful ones are, as well.

Chances are, unless you do something extremely proactive, those annoying, irritating traits are going to remain a part of your leadership story until you take one radical step to change it. And that radical step isn't about changing your behaviour: it's about getting others on board.

Most of my time coaching is spent working with people on their behaviour. Behaviour, quite simply put, is what you walk around saying and doing. Your body language, the actions you take and the words you choose to use are key elements of your behaviour that people will use to evaluate, judge, assume intention and, often, like or dislike you as a result.

I find that the people I coach get very little constructive feedback on their behaviour. I think this is largely because **talking to people about their behaviour can be uncomfortable**; we've never really been taught how to give behavioural feedback (unless you took a psychology course or two in university); and we often hold a belief that behaviours never change, particularly when it comes to adults.

As a result of this, people in organizations who are trying to change behaviour are set up to fail. I can't help but think of Kelly, who had been given feedback that she is always late (for meetings, on deadlines, etc.). It's annoying her boss, peers and direct reports. So, Kelly spent the next two months purposefully being on time for her meetings and making sure she hit her deadlines. At a planning meeting, her boss assigned her a task then jokingly said: "And Kelly, it's really critical that you get this in on time." Her colleagues have a little chuckle, but Kelly is miffed at the comment. She hasn't missed a deadline or been late for a meeting in two months! Why is she still being labelled as "the late girl?"

Here's why: Kelly didn't take the radical step of TELLING PEOPLE that she was going to change her behaviour. Instead, she just quietly soldiered on and then got frustrated when people didn't recognize her attempts.

Here's the thing about changing behaviours: it doesn't really matter what you try, if those around you don't see the results. In my experience, attempting to do things differently and changing your behaviour is only half the equation. The other, and possibly more important half, is having other people see that you've changed. And to do that, you need to be "up in their grill" about your activities so that they know to look for the new stuff. It takes us a long time to shift our perceptions of others, so doing this quietly – like Kelly did – for two months, isn't necessarily going to have people label her as the "on time/on deadline gal."

Our brains like to keep things in neat little boxes (aka pigeonholes). If I see you as someone who's perpetually late, that's where my brain has put you and wants to keep you, because brains do that. We like routine and habit. We've got so much information and data flying at us on a millisecond to millisecond basis that we need these kinds of structures to stay sane. So, even though you show up for meetings on time for the next two months and were only late once, I'm going to focus on the one time you were late because that's the behaviour that fits in my nice little pigeonholing brain.

To get me to see you in a new light more quickly, you need to get me on board by letting me know VERY CLEARLY that "being on time" is the behaviour that you're working on. Begin by telling me, as your boss, that this is what you're going to work on. Then, in meetings, when you're on time, make a point of making sure I register that. You can be direct ("Here I am! On time!") or simply say, something like "Looks like it's 9 a.m. and time to start. Is there anyone we're still waiting for?" Whatever you say, just make sure I'm seeing that you're on time. In our next one-on-one, share the results (I'm proud to say I've been on time for all my meetings this week/

month, etc.). Keep putting that "I'm an on-time kind of person" message in front of me until I say to you: "Okay, I get it, you're on time. Now let's work on something else!"

This may sound ridiculous and somewhat overkill, but it's all about getting my lazy brain, which has you firmly stuck in a "late guy/gal" pigeonhole, to start seeing your new behaviour. Chances are, you're not going to be on time every time, but I'll cut you more slack that one time you're late if you've successfully managed to shift my perception.

We spend most of our careers thinking about the knowledge we need to acquire or the skills we need to develop. From my vantage point as a coach and leader, what limits our opportunities are the behaviours we either do or don't exhibit and how others view those behaviours.

Lessons from the Dark Side of Personal Branding

Ever since Tom Peters wrote *Brand You* for *Fast Company* in 1997, there has been a steady stream of advice on how mission-critical it is for us to build and manage our personal brands. Consultants make thousands of dollars teaching people how to write their LinkedIn profiles, spin their resumes and control their online presence. But are we overhyping the flash at the expense of substance?

Politicians have become masters of brand management. From John F. Kennedy to Justin Trudeau to Donald Trump, political campaigns are essentially run on brand power. Then, the elected official shows up in office and the majority of the people are disappointed in what they actually do when they get there. I don't think it's really that they're as inept as they seem, it's just that they can't live up to their own extreme hype.

And there lies the big rub around personal branding. **At the end of the day, if you can't live up to your brand promise, like with any "product", your "clients" will be disappointed and eventually, you'll be left on the shelf.** And, the word-of-mouth about you will be "Yeah, great guy, but doesn't deliver."

In my opinion, we seem to be placing an inordinate amount of emphasis around building personal "brands" and not enough around working hard and delivering results. In the old days, your brand was essentially an evolution of your reputation. Today, it feels like personal branding is being used to shortcut the "pay your dues" stage.

I don't disagree that there's a place for "personal branding". You have one, whether you curate it or not and it can be a useful tool to open the door to career opportunities. However, overpromising and underdelivering isn't going to give your brand, or more importantly your career, long-term staying power. Screw it up and your brand equity will erode in an instant.

So, before you overinvest your energy in worrying about whether your personal brand is visible enough, how about making sure you've hit your latest project out of the park?

Dude, Have You Seen My Passion?

I've been doing a lot of thinking recently about the quest many of us are on to "find our passion" or the "work we love". There's a video that's been making the internet rounds that suggests we should all do what we love and not worry about money. Over time, it suggests, if we are pursuing our passion, the money will come. I actually think that's great advice for anyone in their twenties who doesn't have a partner, a mortgage and all the other trappings that we can fall into that tie us by golden handcuffs to work we don't "love". But what about the rest of us? How do we find our passion mid-career?

Here's what I've learned:

1. **Stop thinking about a destination and start thinking about direction.** This starts with paying attention to what you currently enjoy in your work life, even if it's a really small percentage of what you're doing. Don't get hung up on the fact that you don't know where this will take you.

2. **Start looking for ways to grow that little sliver of passion either in your job or in other places.** Volunteer, join a group, ask for more opportunities on the job. See how you can build your competence in this area.

3. **Keep building your competence.** Competence builds confidence, and with confidence come opportunities.

4. **Seize opportunities.** Always say yes to things that allow you to expand on the work you enjoy doing, even if you're uncomfortable doing it. Growth doesn't happen in the comfort zone. Each stretch creates a stronger you and more capacity to take on more of what you love.

5. **Stay focused on your progress.** Don't focus on the fact that you have not reached your ideal job yet. Reflect on all the steps you've taken and progress you've made towards your new career life.

6. **Broaden your attention.** As the expression goes: "Luck happens when preparation meets hard work." Say "yes" more than "no", and see where the path of opportunity leads you.

7. **You always have a choice.** Many of us stay locked into what we don't enjoy because of financial commitments (house, cottage, private schools). I know I did. But here's the thing: at the end of your life, are you going to look back and wish you'd upgraded your car every two years or finished that basement? Or are you going to regret not having tried to build a life of passion and purpose?

In 2000, I started thinking about becoming an entrepreneur. It took me six years and a smack in the head (aka a horrible job move and the death of a mentor) to finally take the leap and follow my passion. It required selling our house, depleting our savings and stopping any "extras" that we'd been used to. For someone who has an intense need for security, it was a tough time. Over a decade into self-employment, I have no regrets. It isn't always an easy journey, but I will never by haunted by the ghost of "What if?"

How about you?

How to Leave a Lousy Job Without Torpedoing a Bridge

In 2010, JetBlue flight attendant Steven Slater was the talk of the water cooler. Slater made global headlines when he pulled the ultimate employee hissy fit after a passenger gave him a hard time. After hurling obscenities at the passenger through the intercom, Slater grabbed a couple of beers and leapt out of the plane by deploying the emergency slide. In a post-script, passengers have since come forward to say that he was the one with the bad attitude and JetBlue executives are having a hard time finding anyone who will corroborate his story. It made me wonder: does torpedoing a career bridge ever make sense?

When news broke about Steven Slater's meltdown, many admired the "take-this-job-and-shove-it" gusto to which he exited his post. In an NBC News poll, 55% of people who completed it cited Slater as a "hero". (24% thought he was just plain crazy.)

Pulling a "Slater" is a fantasy that's probably crossed most people's minds at one time or another, but for leaders who've invested years in building their career reputations, the high from that quick moment of "stickin' it to the man" probably isn't worth it, unless you're planning on leaving your field altogether and setting up a pottery studio in an isolated cabin somewhere.

For those who are not into the Steven Slater career suicide approach, here are a few tips on how to exit gracefully when you've hit the wall:

> **Vent out the emotions.** Before doing anything, find a friend and ask them to give you ten minutes of listening time to let you vent out every horrible, nasty thing you ever wanted to get off your chest about the

stinking, miserable job that you're going to be leaving. There. Doesn't that feel better? If not, repeat process until your head is clear.

Keep it professional. When the time comes to tender your resignation, keep it simple, straightforward and professional. Don't try to over-explain and, given that most people quit because of their relationship with their boss, don't bother trying to offer any "constructive" feedback to your boss at this point. Save that for the exit interview (if there is one).

Keep your nose clean. Once you've handed in your resignation notice, continue to deliver 100% on your commitments. Remember, your last impression will be your legacy. Don't blow a great track record with a lousy final few weeks.

Don't badmouth your employer. Even if you worked for the worst boss in the world, take the high road and don't stoop to slinging mud on your way out. It only makes you look bitter. Plus, the people left behind aren't going to thank you for it.

Maintain strong relationships with external contacts. You may be worried that you'll take the fall on some bad decisions that your bad boss is making. Work hard during your final weeks to make sure your external contacts have nothing but great impressions of working with you. Even if your boss does try to sabotage your reputation, they'll have their own experience to judge you by.

Don't badmouth your employer. This is worth repeating. Do not badmouth your employer, especially if the boss is a triple jerk. Industries are small, and, in my experience, jerk bosses seem to be powerfully adept at managing their external reputations. Don't get into a mud-slinging contest that you might not win.

Put a bow on it. Make sure you complete all your deliverables and leave people with as much information on any outstanding items as you can. They'll remember you going the extra mile to make the transition smooth.

Be constructive. If you have the opportunity to provide feedback during the exit interview, be as constructive as possible – emphasis on the word "constructive". Don't use it as an opportunity to take parting personal pot-shots at your former employer. They probably won't make a difference and may only give your boss the ammunition they need to reinforce that you were really the problem, not them.

For extra bonus points... Provide a one-week transition where people can call you if they have questions – but only for a week. After that, you need to let them move on without you. Set that line clearly in the sand from the beginning.

It's possible that, over the span of your career, you may find yourself in at least one untenable employment situation. Before you deploy the emergency slide and hurl abuse at bystanders on your way out, take a deep breath, phone a friend, get a third opinion and plan your move with a cool head.

As for Slater, years after the incident, he has no regrets. In an interview with Australia's 9 News, he shared how, "on the way down the slide, he felt a 'lightening of the soul' and when he reached the bottom, he felt 'exhilarated and free'." He also said: "I have no regrets and am thankful to be out of an untenable situation with an abusive employer and industry."

So perhaps the other lesson here is, if you're going to go out in flames, really go "all in" on your exit. At least it will give you your 15 minutes of fame.

Leaping Lanes Mid-Career: How to Do It and Not Derail

Confucius said: "Choose a job you love, and you will never have to work a day in your life." Jumping around in your twenties is a great way to figure out what you want to be when you grow up, but what do you do mid-career when you're still on the quest for that dream job?

Here are a few tips on how to make a career lane leap:

Know your assets and your limitations. Be real about what you're good at and what you're not. Solicit feedback from people who know you and who've worked with you to get perspective on what you bring to the table.

Watch out for the comfort effect. In rapidly changing times, your experience may be your own worst enemy. Recognize when you're starting to stagnate. Don't get comfortable. Keep learning and challenging yourself.

Inventory your job satisfaction. Are you really in need of a leap or are you in need of a reality check? Do an annual pros and cons list of what you're loving and hating about your job. Add up the totals and if the dissatisfiers are too big, start to hunt with the knowledge of what you're looking to move towards (vs. what you're trying to move away from).

Don't manage your dream off the side of your desk. Take the time to think through very clearly what drives your career happiness. Allow yourself time to reflect and build your personal career vision.

When you don't fit "on paper", connect the dots. Know what a potential new employer may be looking for. Share stories that create an image that helps people visualize how your skillset fits their requirements.

Know your personal non-negotiables. What are yours? Culture, organization, people, decision-making, opportunities, projects, autonomy, etc. Don't compromise. One of my clients had a non-negotiable about leaving at 4 p.m. to pick up her kids. Another client's related to having a three week vacation each year where he would unplug. Non-negotiables are typically tied closely to your personal values, so start there in thinking about your own.

Be clear on what you're willing to change. By mid-career, you will likely have some elements of your personality or approach that you aren't willing to change or compromise. Recognize what these are and the implications they may have on your job options.

Be honest with yourself and your employer. Consider if you are a start up person, a turn-around person or a steady-state person. Recognize what strengths you bring to the role and what you enjoy doing. Make sure the fit is there both for you and your employer (whether seeking a new role inside or outside your organization).

Think evolution not revolution. Career shifts often happen through a process of learning more about who you are and what you love to do. Broaden your self-awareness, solicit feedback, volunteer to deepen your understanding of new areas and pursue opportunities that extend your network, both inside and outside your organization.

In my experience, it's never too late to try something new. The trick is to be comfortable with the corresponding risk.

Lessons Learned in a Decade of Entrepreneurship

The date was January 9th, 2007. It was my 39th birthday and it was my last day of full-time employment. I remember walking out of the office frantically throwing to-do lists at everyone in my path, completely unsure of what I was about to step into. No plan, no income, no severance, no sugar daddy, no safety net of savings. Here's what I've learned along the way that I think is equally applicable to a new entrepreneur or to a leader on the way up the ladder:

1. **You can do more than what you think you can do.** Everybody is scared shitless and feels like they don't know what they're doing. The difference is that they lean into the fear and push forward. I have to continually remind myself of that fact, which make my fears become increasingly manageable.

2. **When other people believe in you, believe them. Period.** We often hold ourselves so much smaller than we have the potential to be. Listen to those around you. Surround yourself with people who believe in you and will support you.

3. **When you leave your fancy post with the fancy title, you'll really see who your real friends are.** Someone once told me that they were just "renting" their title until the next person came along. Very true, so don't let what it says on your business card define your worth as a person.

4. **There's a lot of bullshit bravado in the entrepreneurial community that you don't have to subscribe to.** You don't have to sacrifice your family to build a business. You don't have to be making millions of dollars to be successful. You don't have to have a fancy office with matching furniture to have "made it".

5. **Just because you run your own business doesn't mean you'll be in a perpetual state of bliss.** There'll be good days, bad days and days that are simply "meh". Whether you're self-employed or have a job you love, not every day is going to be sunshine and lollipops. That's life.

6. **You will face disappointment and rejection.** And you may possibly even have people do unethical things, like steal your clients or rip-off your ideas. But if you continue to care about the work you do and the people you work with, none of that stuff will really matter. You will keep going, growing and making a difference.

7. **"Talk does not cook rice".** Neither does a slick website or cool marketing collateral. Building a business (or a great career) is 100% about the hustle.

8. **You can have too much of a good thing.** Shiny object syndrome is a real affliction and one best controlled by surrounding yourself with people who don't think the way you think. I'm grateful for all the amazing people who have worked with me at The Roundtable over the years and kept me on the straight and narrow (for the most part, anyway!).

9. **Being an entrepreneur is the most stressful job in the world.** There is never a "steady state". You will worry about making payroll, you will worry about where your next client project is coming from, you will worry if your new team member will work out... It's endless. Sometimes a steady paycheque is so much more appealing but...

10. **Being an entrepreneur is the most amazing, rewarding and exciting career in the world.** It has given me the opportunity to connect with so many amazing people. I wouldn't trade it for a second and only wish that I'd had the belief in myself to start the journey sooner.

If you're someone thinking of taking a leap into uncharted territory, whether that be self-employment or a new job or industry, remember: we are much more likely to be driven by our fears, and that's what ultimately holds us back. Don't let your fears get in your way. Take the leap and pursue whatever dream you might be chasing.

#AVOID CAREER PITFALLS

A problem for many successful people, in my observation, is knowing when to let go of the need to win. That high drive to achieve results gets translated into all aspects of work life (and even home life) and we can find ourselves winning the small battles but losing the war. Winning comes in a variety of forms and, if you're naturally competitive, you may not even realize just how much you're trying to win all the time. Here are some thoughts: let someone else own the idea. Let another department get the head count. Learn to compromise. The long-term effects of building collaborative partnerships and relationships will far outweigh the short-term win of the argument.

5 Dumb Reasons Why Smart Leaders Derail

The problem with being smart and successful is that, well, you're smart and successful. It really is possible to have too much of a good thing in one's career. Case in point: Oprah Winfrey. After dominating the afternoon ratings, Winfrey decided to launch a network. Not a new show. A whole TV network. It didn't go the way she planned. If even titans like Winfrey can have a career misstep, so can all of us little people.

There are countless books written on why people fail, but in my experience (both personally and from working with a variety of leaders over the past two decades), there are five key factors that seem to consistently trip people up:

1. **Overestimating the importance of IQ.** For anyone who believes that they'll be a successful leader because they're smart, here's the news-flash: only if you're über "Elon Musk" smart. The rest of us need EQ. IQ is what gets you to the table. It's your ability to work with others – emotional intelligence (EQ) or "how" you lead – that will make you successful.

2. **Underestimating the importance of culture.** I've said it before and I'll say it again: culture will eat strategy for lunch and it will eat leaders, too. The more senior you get, the more important it is that you have the ability to navigate the politics and relationships that drive an organization's culture.

3. **The Syndromes of Superhero and Imposter.** Superheroes take on more and more and can't say "no". They stretch themselves until they start derailing on the things that they used to be good at, and end up burning out and getting bitter. Imposters are driven by the fear

of being "found out". They can derail by creating a self-fulfilling prophecy of sabotage.

4. **Believing your own hype.** Too much success can create out of control egos (delusions of significance). You start to believe you're untouchable, unbeatable. You ignore trends, emerging technologies and changes in client needs. You get stuck resting on the fumes of prior success.

5. **Overusing strengths.** Overused strengths become liabilities, and relying on leadership techniques that worked well for you at one level of leadership may be less effective at another.

As you enter mid-career, the stakes get higher and missteps get costlier. Being proactive can help you avoid costly career-limiting moves and enjoy increased career success throughout your mid-career and beyond.

> Check out page 167 and get a **FREE** Bonus program to help you avoid these derailers and bullet proof your career!

The Downside of Hitching Your Wagon to a Shiny Star

The leadership train wreck of 2016 was, hands down, Donald J. Trump's run for the Presidency in the United States. His leadership foibles have been documented ad nauseam, so I'm not going to go there. Instead, I thought I'd take a look at his number one advocate and hanger-on, his daughter, Ivanka. The question that runs through my mind is: "Will Ivanka's career survive after the Trump presidency?"

Early on in my career, I worked for a guy who painted himself as a bit of a superstar, a veritable corporate saviour. One day, he said to me: "Listen, don't hitch your star to my wagon." (Um... well, actually, I hadn't been, but this guy wasn't short on ego, either.)

Regardless, the advice stuck in my head. He left the organization the following year and, sure enough, the "new boss" wasn't anything like the "old boss" and by default (having been hired by the "old boss"), I was no longer enjoying the "inner circle" status I'd once held.

Over my career, I've watched many leaders align themselves to "superstars" and high fliers with varying results. In some cases, when the superstar leaves, they take the hanger-on with them (further cementing the hanger-on's reputation as one of not being able to stand on their own two feet). In other cases, and particularly if the superstar was also a pain in the behind (aka Trump), the hanger-on who stays behind quickly gets thrown under the bus.

Riding on someone else's career's coattails may get you ahead in the short-term, but it's highly unlikely that it will keep your career on track over the long haul. It's probably time to let go of the apron strings and stand on your own two feet.

Let's see what happens to Ivanka Trump (and all the other Trump hang-er-ons) when the dust settles. My guess is that Trump himself will come out relatively unscathed, but those around him may bear the brunt of other people's disdain for many years to come.

Stuck in the Middle - Is Ageism Stalling Your Move Up the Ladder?

A disturbing pattern may be coming to a job opportunity near you. For first wave Gen X leaders born between 1964 and 1974, a new twist on the old "you need work experience to get a job, but to get the experience, you need the job" tail chaser seems to be emerging. This time it's called "to get that VP role, you need to be in a VP role."

In the past few months, I've had multiple conversations with Director level executives in their early 40s who've been passed over for VP roles. The conversations go like this: "Well, I wanted to apply for the job but my [boss/president/head-hunter] told me that I needed VP level experience to be considered as an applicant."

What the what??

Here's the issue as I see it: Baby Boomers who climbed through the ranks ahead of Gen X and Gen Y were able to hit VP level roles in their 30s, and then they sat there... and sat there... and sat there. This essentially allowed very few Gen X leaders the opportunity to move beyond the Director level because there simply wasn't anywhere to move up. This has essentially wiped out a decade of progressive leadership experience amongst those in the early part of the Gen X cohort.

Here's the kicker. Now that leadership ranks are opening up a little, organizations are looking down into their leadership bench to see who they should be plucking out to put on the "succession" track to fill these senior level roles, and they may be jumping over the 40 and early 50 somethings in favour of younger leaders.

Think about it. If you are a 43-year-old Director, interviewing with a 55-year-old Boomer leader who made VP when s/he was 35, don't you think that they may be a little bit biased? After all, if they made VP in their 30s, shouldn't you already be there by now?

Titles are funny things. They don't seem to matter until they matter. If you're trying to make the leap from Director to VP and are over 36 or so, here's the memo: the game has changed. Now that you're no longer the "fresh-faced up-and-comer", you may need to think differently about how you position yourself to climb up the next rung.

For those under 35ish, my advice is to rack up the experience and titles you need to get the opportunities you deserve in the next decade. After 35, you stop being "cute" and the windows of opportunity seem to become harder to find. Plus, the older we get, the less likely we are to want to compromise our values or change our approach (My friend once said to me when sharing why she quit her job, "Fuck you, I'm 40" which loosely translated means: I'm just not willing to compromise on certain things anymore. This mindset – although totally understandable – may leave fewer opportunities on the table for a mid-career job hunter).

Talent is talent and shouldn't be defined by age. It's a good reminder for all of us to be aware of our own biases and what expectations we're placing on those around us. We may be limiting the career potential of others and not even know it.

The Top 5 Warning Signs You're About to Be Fired

Have you ever noticed that sometimes it's much easier to see the train wrecks that are about to happen to someone else's careers before your own? I just finished reading Lindsay Lohan's interview in *Vanity Fair* where she insists that she can rebuild her career and achieve the potential that everyone thought she had. It got me thinking how, when you've been a superstar performer, it's hard to face the reality that your career is off the rails (and that most people saw it coming way before you did!).

I began to reflect on the warning signs. How do you know that your fast-tracking leadership career is about to end with an escort to the door? Here are some of the things to look out for:

1. **You're no longer in the loop.** You used to be the go-to guy or gal and now, other people seem to know more than you do. Ramp this up to red alert if one of those people in the know is the part-time office cleaner.

2. **Your boss stops dropping by your office to chat.** In fact, he seems to avoid walking past your office all together. Double alert if he's lunching with that "friendly" new guy that's been nosing around your department.

3. **The "friendly" new guy is getting in your business.** Citing his "prior experience", he makes a business case to take over part of your department… and wins. Yup. Definitely a sign that there's a new golden boy in town. Once you start losing scope, it's a good guess that something's amuck.

4. **Your inner circle peers stop making eye contact with you in meetings.** You notice that your suggestions seem to be passed over and subtly (or not so subtly) ignored. Oh, except for when that friendly new guy makes them. Can you hear the time bomb ticking?

5. **They add a new position to your team that you knew nothing about, and the person they hired seems WAY too qualified.** Chances are this guy's your successor and is just waiting to learn the ropes before you get shown the door. This is guaranteed if he went to school with the "friendly new guy". Might as well start packing your box at this point.

There you go. If you see some of these signs happening around you, my advice is to go and have a heart-to-heart with your boss to see what's real and what's just your paranoia. After all, what's worse? Not knowing where you stand and tanking out your self-esteem while you wait for the axe to fall, or securing a nice severance and moving on to your next big opportunity?

I know which poison I'd choose to drink.

The Gig Triangle: 2 out of 3 Ain't Bad. Or Is It?

My husband is a bass player and, many years ago, educated me on the term "gig triangle" to explain his dissatisfaction with a particular band he was playing in. According to an article he'd read in *Bass Player Magazine* for a band to rock, you have to have great tunes, great money and great hang (bandmates). According to the author of the original article, two out of three are enough to make it workable.

I've been thinking about the gig triangle for a while and how it relates to those of us working stiffs, and I'm questioning whether two out of three is actually sustainable. Here's why: when you think about our world of work, the gig triangle adapts a little to be more like this: great money, great work and great environment (people/culture/work space). With two out of three factors being a hit, your inner voice may go something like this:

- I can put up with these twits because I'm doing what I love and they're paying me fantastically well! (money/work)

- Even though the money's not great, I love my colleagues and every day feels like play because I'm doing what I LOVE, LOVE, LOVE! (work/environment)

- I may not be doing exactly what I want to do, but the money is awesome and the people I work with are fantastic. I'll pursue my real passion in my side business. (money/environment)

Having lived through several of those two out of three career incarnations myself, my opinion is that **you can put up with two out of three for a while, but chances are, you're not going to be able to put up with it for long.** Something's going to have to give.

You may be able to put up with twits or a lousy work culture for a while, but eventually all the money in the world and the fact that you like your job isn't going to make it worth the stress or toll that it's probably taking on your health. If you love your job and the people you work with but the money is limiting your options in the lifestyle department, eventually you may need to move on and make other choices. And, if you're pursuing your real passion/talents outside of work because you can't do it at work, that may eventually turn into your new full-time gig.

I also think that things aren't weighted evenly. Most bands will break up because of "bad hang". When I talk to leaders who are miserable, it's usually because of the lousy work environment. In fact, the #1 reason people leave jobs is because of their relationship with their boss. That's all about bad hang.

Bands like Kiss and the Rolling Stones may be able to sustain the gig triangle with two out of three things being covered because the money is outrageous and they don't have to "hang" together for long periods of time, just for a few tour dates. For a short-term project, the two out of three mantras may work, but any longer and chances are, you'll be moving on.

So, how's your gig triangle? Are you living a 1/3, 2/3 or 3/3 career life? What's the conversation you need to have to get a better balance? After all, you only get one go-around in this lifetime, so you might as well make it the best it can be.

The Career Doom Loop: Are You on a Slippery Slope?

Years ago, I was introduced to this great model called "The Career Doom Loop". The concept was created by Charles Jett and popularized in Dory Hollander's book *The Doom Loop System*. It's a simple model that stuck in my head and made my own career path make so much more sense. It goes like this:

When you first start a new position, you are in stage 1 of the "doom loop". You are in a job you LIKE/that you're NOT GOOD at. Goes to reason; when you start out, you don't even know where the photocopier is, never mind how to contribute to your best ability.

Which then leads us to stage 2. You are in a job you LIKE/that you are GOOD AT. You've hit your stride, you're contributing, your employer adores you.

Which then leads to the next stage and the time when the "doom looping" begins. You are in a job you DON'T like/that you are GOOD AT. Ah yes, the boredom factor has kicked in. You're still good, but you're starting to check out.

Which is when one of two things will usually happen:

1. You continue to slide to the final stage of the "doom loop": you don't like your job/you're no longer good at it. You've probably seen this around organizations. It's often called "dead wood".

2. If you are a high performing fast tracker, you'll never even hit the fourth and final stage. You will likely pop yourself out of your

organization and head to greener pastures where you can begin again at stage one in a job you like, but that you're not great at yet.

And there, my friends, lies the lesson. If you are currently managing a fast tracker, don't stick your head in the sand when you see the boredom factor setting in. To keep these ambitious types engaged, you have to throw them into a situation that they're excited about but not good at yet. Yes, this might mean transferring them to another department to get a new set of experiences, and that means you're going to have to deal with a hole in your team, but really, isn't that better than them walking out the door and taking all their IP to your competitor?

And, if you are said fast tracker, here's the thing to think about. If you're working for a boss who hasn't read your boredom and/or doesn't have the wherewithal to issue a new challenge, why not try suggesting one to them yourself? After all, the grass always looks greener when you're getting stuck in a career rut. But sometimes, our best opportunities can be found right under our noses, if we're just willing to look.

LEAD WITH PURPOSE

Section 2

#SET YOUR DIRECTION

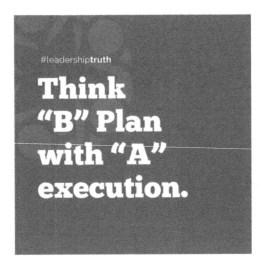

Over the years of leading teams and building a business, I've noticed one of the biggest killers of progress is the quest for perfection. I've watched teams try to figure out the perfect plan before executing their ideas only to find themselves missing the opportunity. With the world changing at ever increasing speeds, the best thing you can do is ship your ideas; get them quickly out the door. Once they're out in the world, test, learn, adjust and refine. I had a boss that used to call this "Changing the fan belt while the motor is running." For entrepreneurs, this concept is second nature. For more risk-adverse organizations, it's time to worry less about developing the perfect 'A' plan and more about executing a 'B' plan well.

Wisdom from Winston Churchill

On October 22nd, 2011, my father passed away after a short, but vigorous, battle with cancer. My dad was a larger-than-life guy and, of great comfort to my mum, brothers and myself was the outpouring of memories we received from his former pupils, rugby lads, friends and lawn bowling buddies. One of my dad's favourite quotes is attributed to Winston Churchill:

"You make a living by what you get. You make a life by what you give."

Standing in my parents' living room, looking at all the "things" my dad had acquired over the course of his lifetime (he was a real pack rat) was a stark reminder of the phrase "You can't take it with you". Seeing his slippers by his chair, reading 60 year-old excuse notes from parents asking Mr. Roberts to let their sons out of P.E. class, and looking at his collection of rugby awards and memorabilia made us smile. But it was the notes we received from the people whose lives he somehow helped to shape that gave us the most comfort.

My dad was a natural leader. I learned many lessons from him about hard work, taking risks and questioning misplaced authority. Through the many notes of condolence, we heard how my dad had inspired others, including former players, pupils and colleagues, to pursue their dreams and ambitions. Many of them credited their successes later in life to lessons they'd learned from my dad on the rugby pitch.

My dad wasn't a big celebrity (although he probably could have been in the world of sport if he'd cared a toss for that kind of thing, which he didn't). He just loved what he did and cared about the people he was leading as a coach. Sure, he was a hard-ass and could be impatient and tough. But you always knew that my dad was in your corner cheering you on and believing in you.

This is what life really is all about: the ultimate legacy of what you leave behind is what you leave with others. What a wonderful opportunity we all have to make a lasting, positive difference in the lives of other people. I hope you are making the most of your opportunities to build your legacy every day, just like my dad did.

The Age of Deception: How to Avoid the Lying Game

It seems everywhere we turn these days, we're surrounded by liars. And I don't just mean "alternative facts" type liars. Statistics suggest that over 50% of people lie on their resumes. Whether by inflating their titles, accomplishments or academic credentials, it appears many of us apply for jobs with the assumption that our best isn't going to be good enough. All this lying got me wondering why being honest is so difficult.

A friend of mine's husband is a professional cyclist and good friends with one of the members of Lance Armstrong's team. A lot has been written about the pressure Armstrong put on his teammates to dope up, but why did people ultimately do it? It's easy to say it comes down to a set of personal ethics, but in my observation, ethics seem to get very blurry when the temptation placed before us is impossible to resist and we're surrounded by people who make the "wrong choice" seem OK.

For a professional cyclist who knows that doping is rampant amongst the sport, I think it would be very tough to resist the temptation of succumbing to peer pressure if it ultimately meant walking away from your personal dreams and ambitions. Our minds have a funny way of justifying things when you're trying to get what you want and are surrounded by people telling you it's OK.

In corporate life, how else can you explain CEOs who can justify multimillion dollar salaries for themselves while squeezing the hell out of front-line and middle management? This isn't good, ethical behaviour, but it's become normalized because Boards and senior leaders have lied themselves into believing that they are somehow worth more than 300 times the average frontline leader's salary.

When former CEO of Groupon Andrew Mason wrote this exit message to employees, he made some serious headlines: "After four and a half intense and wonderful years as CEO of Groupon, I've decided that I'd like to spend more time with my family. Just kidding – I was fired today. If you're wondering why, you haven't been paying attention." The message caused a stir both inside and outside the business world for its brutal honesty and made me wonder: what type of world and workplaces are we creating where honesty makes headlines?

It seems that bullshit has become the norm. It feels like every other headline is about somebody fabricating something. Whether it's a president lying about an election win, a high profile public education professional plagiarizing articles, leaders lying about their credentials, famous sports stars lying about doping, or the average individual inflating their resumes, it seems like we're all suffering from massive amounts of insecurity.

We're becoming an entire culture of "I'm not good enough!" and it's hard to get away from it.

Now, I don't think that most leaders set out to become liars in the same way pot smokers don't plan to become meth addicts. I think it's a slow, slippery slope that starts to gain momentum over time, with the right conditions. It often starts with "innocent" little white lies like this:

"Sorry, I'm late. My printer wasn't working." *(Actually, the printer was fine, I just spent too much time jamming in "one more thing" before the meeting.)*

"We'll definitely consider your proposal." *(No, we won't, because we have an incumbent vendor that we really like but we needed to go through a bid exercise to appease the Board.)*

"You're doing a good job." *(Actually, you're doing an OK job and we'd like to replace you, but we don't want to tell you that because we don't want you to quit until we get through a busy period.)*

"I love that idea." *(I hate that idea, but I won't tell you that. Instead, I'll just let it languish and nothing will come of it.)*

Don't think you're a liar? Here's an interesting exercise: try tracking the number of times in a day where you exaggerate, tell a "little white lie" or omit information (which is like lying by omission). Then reflect on why you were lying. I tried it and found that, for me, in many cases my lies were all in an effort to protect my personal image over extremely stupid things. Being conscious of the triggers that caused me to lie has made me more aware of it and got me thinking: if we all got a handle on the small lies, maybe we'd be in better shape to avoid telling the world (and ourselves) the really big whoppers. What do you think?

What Makes a Great Leader?

One of my favourite management tools is Situational Leadership. If you don't know it, Google it; it's terrific. I love simple concepts that stand the test of time and the Blanchard/Hersey model is just that. But, like anything else, it can boil down to nothing more than a pretty picture if you don't do something with your new knowledge. Which brings me to a great quote from Erwin McManus:

"The world doesn't need more great leaders, it needs more great people who lead." - Erwin McManus

The quote made me pause and think: what makes someone great? The greatest people I've seen – not just in leadership, but in life – never think they're great, but they all seem to share one simple trait: they want to do and be better.

They never seem to feel like they've got it all figured out and, as leaders, are continually looking for ways to improve.

The bottom line is that models like Situational Leadership aren't going to make you a better leader. They are just tools. It's your ability to use the tools that makes them worth knowing. And this really boils down to your own level of self-insight and willingness to build the skills and behaviours (which is harder) that you need to be better. The more you understand yourself, the better you can lead others.

So, if you want to be a great leader who leads with purpose, I suggest that you start by confronting your shortcomings and uncovering your blind spots, relentlessly. Although hearing negative feedback is never pleasant, the more you become aware of your assets and liabilities, the more power you have to do something about them and get the leadership opportunities you want and deserve.

Build Your Confidence in One 'Easy' Step

Lately I've been thinking that the toughest job for most leaders is maintaining positivity and confidence in a relentless environment of uncertainty. The pressure put on most leaders to continue to deliver results hasn't let up. All this pressure can sap your energy and confidence, making it very difficult to rally the troops come Monday morning. If you're feeling battle-fatigued, here's a quick exercise you can try to get your team's (and your own) energy flowing in the right direction:

Start talking about the positives.

There. That's it. It may sound too simple, but give it a try. Here's how:

If your team is down in the dumps, push the momentum in another direction by starting every single one of your team meetings by asking each member for one thing that happened in the past week that was positive. If they can't think of anything professionally, ask them to share a personal story.

Keep doing it every time you get together. You will be amazed at how much this starts to send the energy in your group in a better direction.

If you're personally struggling with how to stay positive, do the same thing. At the end of each work day, jot down five things that were positive for you that day. Big or small, it doesn't matter. It's about putting your focus on the positive vs. the negative. After doing it for a week, you'll be amazed at how much stronger and more resilient you'll feel.

Your mindset is a powerful thing. Use it to your advantage.

#NAVIGATE TURBULENCE

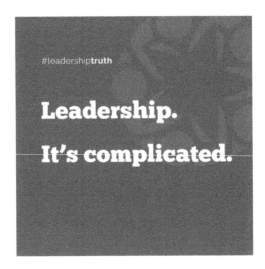

#leadership**truth**

Leadership.

It's complicated.

Whenever people tell me they want to be a leader, I always ask them 'why'? Leadership isn't easy. It's usually pretty thankless. People will always have a list of things you should be doing better. And, of course, what's on some people's lists (listen better) is not on others (speak up more). Leadership is a rollercoaster ride of highs and lows. When things go right, your team will get the credit but when things go wrong, you'll take the blame. And by the way, everyone will tell you that you should be happy about that (when inside, you're in need of recognition as much as the next person). Yes, leadership is gratifying. It's amazing to see people blossom and to be able to guide and shape direction. I absolutely love leading, but I would be lying if I didn't say that there are days when I wish I didn't feel as passionately about leadership. It might make life a little less complicated.

Leadership Competency to Avoid: Hysteria

Anytime a major snowfall hits my hometown of Toronto, someone invariably will begin reminiscing about the memorable winter of January 1999 when our then Mayor Mel Lastman called in the army. The sight of an armoured tank rolling down the middle of Yonge Street isn't something I'll ever forget. Ridiculed by the rest of Canada as overreacting, headlines like the following made the front pages: *Toronto calls in army; rest of Canada calls it winter.*

This reaction was in a long line of decisions and actions that Mel Lastman took to cement his reputation as a bit of a crackpot, and certainly clouded any good work that he did do in the mayoral seat.

As leaders, we get judged on all the actions we take. One dumb move can wipe out at least three to five smart moves you've made and take you much longer to recover from. String a number of dumb moves together (as with Lastman) and you'll find yourself spending a long, long time digging out of the reputation mud.

Studies show that if your first impression of someone is highly positive, they will have to screw up three times before you will change your opinion of them. The reverse is also true. If you screw up in a big way, then you'll need to be spectacular at least three times before someone will change their opinion of you. Emphasis on the word spectacular.

So, next time you need to make a decision in a time of crisis, keep your reputation intact and:

- **Surround yourself with a diverse group of advisors who understand the issues fully and are as "agenda-free" as possible.** Hysteria can often create groupthink as people get caught up in the negative energies

95

and emotions being created. This is especially true when people don't understand or have all the facts.

- **Listen to your intuition.** Don't be bullied into making decisions that you don't feel are right. After the dust settles, you'll be the one blamed or lauded for whatever you decided to do, so you might as well pick the route that you can live with.

- **Take a deep breath and press pause.** Sometimes, when those around you are shrieking for a quick decision, it's easy to get caught up in acting without thinking. Slow down and get as many facts as you can.

- **Step back and re-evaluate.** Is the crisis real or is it imagined? Sometimes work can take on mythic proportions when the reality is, by slowing down, circumstances may change and the crisis may not really be a crisis after all. Don't forget: most of the pressure we put on ourselves is internal.

And, whatever you do, don't whine to the media about how you just want your life back as a certain BP CEO did once upon a time. Just like hysteria, whining is not part of any leader's job description.

Self-Deprecation to Self-Sabotage: It's a Fine Line

I learned a very important lesson last week: when someone asks you what you felt you did well, do not, under any circumstances, launch into a laundry list of self-criticism. Sure, it's good to be able to identify your own areas for improvement, but when you're being asked what worked and instead start sharing what didn't, all you're doing is putting the focus on the negative and sabotaging yourself.

When I launched The (then Executive) Roundtable in 2008, I opened my first PowerRoundtable session by thanking my friend who had hosted the event for me at her swanky club. I jokingly said: "I'm thankful she is a member, because I sure couldn't afford a membership here!" Afterwards, my friend Mel (who, I may add, is never short on feedback), said to me "Stop with that self-deprecating stuff. You don't need it and it just takes away from your success." (It may have been a bit more colourful than that, but you get the picture.)

It was awesome feedback and I'm grateful that she shared it with me. Her point was that I had a room full of people who wanted to be part of something that was "winning", and not feeling that they were in a group that was financially sketchy.

Interestingly, a couple of months later, I ended up joining that same club. Through the process of joining, the owner talked to me about how difficult it was to attract new members. Each time I bumped into her, that same theme kept emerging, and it made me wonder: "Why is nobody joining? Have I made a mistake? Is this club really viable or have I just taken a big gamble?"

Self-sabotage typically occurs because – at some level – our brain is trying to keep us (our ego) "safe". In my case, joking about my financial position early into the launch of my business may have been a way to make myself feel better should the business stall, or was possibly a reflection of my own fear of "not being good enough" to be an entrepreneur.

Self-sabotage often starts with that pesky inner critic whispering things like "this presentation isn't going to go well. You didn't prepare enough." You then hit the stage and open with a remark like this: "I'm looking forward to today's presentation, but I have to let you know, I didn't have a lot of time to prepare so please keep that in mind as we move through. There was more that I would have done if I'd had a bit more time." Essentially, you've planted the expectation that you're not prepared which will cause people to look for your shortcomings. Then when you get feedback after the presentation that your content was a bit light, you've then lived up to your "promise".

Having a sense of humour about your failings and foibles isn't a bad thing. Just be mindful that you're not crossing over that fine line between self-deprecation and self-sabotage. Work is tough enough as it is. You don't need to add to the pressure by getting in your own way!

How to Pull Yourself out of the Pit of Despair

They were going to be Canada's Retail Saviour. When Target announced their plans to expand north of the border, bargain shoppers from coast to coast rejoiced. I was lucky enough to work with their top senior talent for close to a year, so it was truly heartbreaking for me when the United States Parent Company decided to abruptly close down operations. I watched as these wonderful leaders had to let go of the dreams and aspirations they had when they joined that company two short years prior.

As I listened to them talk through their experience at our leadership program's closing session, I asked them to reflect on what positive experiences they had gained from their time at Target. Their insights were beautiful, impactful and generous. Even though they were sad, angry and hurting, each leader managed to find laughter, gratitude and inspiration. This experience made me think of how easy it is, especially when times are difficult, to lose sight of all we've accomplished and gained.

As human beings, we have a wonderful capacity to focus on what we didn't do, what we had left to do, how we screwed things up, how we're inadequate compared to others, etc., etc. It's so painful!

But it's also preventable. **One of the things I've learned is that the key to happiness and contentment is to focus on what you've accomplished instead of focusing on the space between where you are now and where you wish you were.** Recognizing your progress, accomplishments and growth, all create positive feelings and can put negative situations in a better perspective. It doesn't mean that the tough stuff is going to go away, but it does mean that you will be able to strengthen your mindset and navigate the rough waters more easily.

So, when you find yourself suddenly with the rug pulled out from under you through a layoff, a horrible professional misstep or some other perceived shortfall, try this:

1. Reflect on what you've accomplished over the course of your career that makes you proud; list your successes; list your progress. Nothing is too small. Ignore the voice that may say "well, that was just doing your job." Bullshit. It's progress; capture it!

2. Think about the people you've helped; think about the successful relationships you've built.

3. Think about how far you've come from that person you were 6, 12 and 18 months ago – then, 6, 12 and 18 years ago.

Now take a deep breath. Doesn't that feel better? Look at all that you've done! You're AMAZING! All these talents and experiences are going to come forward with you, whatever your next adventure may be. How fabulous is that?!

GROW YOUR PEOPLE

Section 3

#MANAGE YOURSELF

Let's face it: everyone has bad days. It's easy to be a wonderful leader when things are going well and life is flowing. It's harder to manage our "dark side" behaviours when we're under stress or pressure. As someone who spends 90% of my time thinking about leadership (the other 10% is spent on bookkeeping), I still screw up fairly regularly. You're not always going to get it right. Some days you're going to be the version of yourself that you like the least. What works for me is to pay attention and be aware of the things that triggered me and learn from that. Then be kind to yourself. Tomorrow is a new day and, as Maya Angelou famously said: "When you know better, you can do better."

When 80% Isn't Good Enough

Recently, I read a tip of the day from a self-proclaimed "leadership guru" that said: "Leadership is about being positive at least 80% of the time." Really? That means I get a full day of being negative every week? I don't usually vehemently disagree with this type of stuff, but this one did set me off a bit.

Here's why: When you're a leader, being positive 80% of the time simply isn't good enough. Now, I recognize that we're all going to have some days that are better than others and, frankly, it's OK from time to time to be a bit down with your team. After all, that's called being human and empathizing with how tough things might be. But don't stay in that pity party pit for too long. The job of a leader isn't to play around in the mud with your team when times are crappy; it's to pull your team out of the mud.

Positivity is one area where you really should be aiming for 99.9%. And that can be hard, especially on days when you're being hammered by your bosses for being behind on goals or when that challenging individual wreaks havoc (yet again) on your well-made plans. The reality is this: leadership can be tough. It's not always fun and it's not always easy. However, the tone you set with your team is the culture you create.

At the end of the day, as Maya Angelou wisely observed, people will remember how you made them feel. In my experience, even if you made them feel great 80% of the time they worked with you, they'll actually remember the 20% that you didn't do so well. And that's the sad fact.

Please aim higher than 80%. But don't try to go it alone; sounding boards, peer groups, coaches and other supports can give you the outlet you need to let off steam so that you can bring your best energy to your colleagues.

Manager as a Coach: Can You Really Be Agenda-Free?

One of the best kept secrets for any leader (in my opinion) is having an external coach. I continue to be amazed by the numbers of leaders who still don't hire coaches for themselves and/or think of it as some "remedial" service that should only be tapped into for people who suck. On the contrary, in my own experience, the people who actually benefit the most from coaching are the people who are already good at what they do, are self-aware and self-motivated. One of the best things about external coaches is their ability to be neutral and agenda free. This got me thinking about whether managers can ever truly be great coaches to their direct reports – especially when it comes to career conversations.

Take this for example: your star employee tells you he doesn't know if he aspires to the role that you have been tracking him towards. This is a huge problem for you, because your own "next move" is dependent on having a successor ready to step up and fill your shoes. This person is your only candidate.

Given that scenario, as their manager, can you really listen without judgment as they explore career options with you? Can you remain neutral as they explain why being a VP of your division may not line up with their own ambitions? (Key words here being MAY NOT.)

I think that's really tough to do. It's certainly a great credit to you if your reports are willing to have such candid conversations about their career struggles, but once that seed of doubt about their ambitions has been planted, can we managers honestly step back and not move into a defensive position? Although you want to help your employee figure out what they really want to be when they grow up, you also have to think about the health of your division and team.

Striking a balance between the needs of the individual and the needs of the organization is something that every manager as coach has to be able to do. But it's certainly not easy. Keeping our own personal agendas in check is probably one of the biggest pitfalls that we have to be aware of in order to be successful. Some progressive organizations like *The Motley Fool* have pulled coaching conversations about career paths away from their managers. Instead, they've trained up a team of line leaders to be internal career coaches. Any employee can go and speak to any of these coaches about their career concerns at any time. I think that's smart.

In today's talent-driven economy, your best performers are going to expect these types of candid, partnership-based conversations. I really think it requires a new mindset towards our role as coaches and one that we all need to figure out how to navigate in order to engage and retain our key talent.

Are You an Insensitive Dummy Like Me?

About 20 years ago, a colleague and I attended a tradeshow on workplace training (we were scouting competitors). One of the vendors was hawking a personality assessment that pinpointed whether you were a Type A, B, C or D person (yes… apparently there is more than Type A). Based on your input, you received a ranking from 1 to 15 on a set of items like inquisitiveness, communication, competitiveness, etc. One of the items was "Sensitivity". I scored 2 out of 15. Needless to say (as with most times we get self-assessment results that we don't like), I was indignant. I'd always felt that I was a fairly caring person who was empathetic to the plights of others. But here's how the conversation went:

Interpreter Guy: It's 3 p.m. and your assistant is working on finalizing a crucial document that has to get out the door by 4:30 p.m. She comes into your office and tells you that her child's school just called and she has to go and pick him up straight away. What's your immediate reaction?

Low Sensitivity Me: Well, I would think about who we could get to finish up the report so that she could get out of there to get her son.

Interpreter Guy: Exactly. That's a great low sensitivity answer.

He turned to my colleague (who had scored 10 out of 15 on the sensitivity scale).

Interpreter Guy: What would you do?

High Sensitivity Colleague (who, for the record, was a guy): I'd ask her what was wrong with her son.

My big aha from all this (and all of you high sensitivity people can stop rolling your eyes right now) was that sensitivity to people's emotional states and empathy for said states are two very different things. I know, duh. But obviously this was a huge blind spot for me. Since then, I have endeavoured to get better at being more sensitive to others, but I have to say (and my husband would probably validate this), it doesn't come easy. I guess it's just not how I'm wired. (How's that for a stereotype buster? Aren't women supposed to be wired for sensitivity?)

I used to work with someone who felt that increasing your sensitivity to others wasn't worth the effort. She felt that you were either wired that way or weren't. After being at it for over 10 years now, I tend to disagree. If you're like me and want to improve your sensitivity or empathy towards others, here are some ideas from my own attempts:

1. **Start paying a lot of attention to your listening and observation skills.** Most leaders I know are really good talkers. Great leaders are really good listeners. Focusing on shifting my behaviour from talking a lot and listening a little, to listening more and talking less, has really helped me better tune in to how what I'm saying is "landing" with other people.

2. **Sometimes you just have to suck it up and get out of your own comfort zone.** I was always happy to tackle work problems and talk about work stuff, but I generally avoided anything that was too personal (read emotional) in nature. So, even when I saw that people were upset about something, I used to try to plough through to keep things focused on business. Now I check-in more to see how they're feeling. And it's actually not that difficult or uncomfortable.

3. **Take a coaching course** (and I don't mean a business-type performance coaching course). Taking a real coaching program that teaches you skills to listen at a deeper and higher level will help you to focus on others.

4. **Take an improvisation class.** If a bonafide coaching program is just way too warm and fuzzy for you, try improvisation. It's all about

listening and communicating and definitely helped me get out of my own agenda and think about others.

I think being insensitive to how your messages or behaviours are impacting others is one of the things that can really reduce your overall impact as a leader. Thankfully, it's something that's "fixable" if you work at it. What do you other insensitive dummies think about that?

Likeability: Yet Another Leadership Issue to Worry About

I recently read my friend Chris Taylor's Actionable book summary of *Likeonomics* by Rohit Bhargava. I haven't read the book, but Chris's crew always does a great job of summarizing the nuggets. And, in this one, research has shown that most of us would rather work for an incompetent fool (aka a nice person who doesn't know what they're doing) than a competent jerk (aka a nasty person who gets the job done). Likeability, it seems, trumps competence when it comes to leaders. And, *Likeonomics* is yet another example of why most business books on leadership irritate me.

Rohit Bhargava isn't the first guy to talk about likeability. Tim Sanders wrote a book called *The Likeability Factor* several years ago that looked at the same thing. In Sanders' book, he also talked about the fact that if you're more likeable, you'll have a happier life. To be likeable, you need to enhance four elements of your personality:

> **Friendliness:** Your ability to communicate and openness to others.
>
> **Relevance:** Your capacity to connect with others' interests, wants and needs.
>
> **Empathy:** Your ability to recognize, acknowledge and experience other people's feelings.
>
> **Realness:** The integrity that stands behind your likeability and guarantees its authenticity.

All well and good, but here's the problem with this "likeability" thing as I see it: what about human chemistry and self-insight? Why is it that some people you automatically like and others you automatically dislike? I, for example, have always really liked people who are a little "left of center", who don't fit the norm, who are a little bit challenging. I like people who are loud and opinionated and aren't afraid to show a little passion for what they believe in. I have a couple of former colleagues who drove most of my coworkers insane because of their powerful presence. I loved them. I thought they were fun and dynamic and energizing. Their clients loved them too. To me, they were highly likeable and yet, to others, they were a bit too loud and brash and over the top.

This leads me to self-insight. As I have learned (thanks to Deepak Chopra), you tend to like people who are like you. You connect with the positive qualities that you want to be true about yourself, that reflect back to you in other people. I want to be seen as someone who is passionate, so therefore I am naturally attracted to people who demonstrate passion, etc.

The counter perspective is also true. If you think of someone that displays qualities that you dislike (think of them right now: what are five things you dislike about them?), well guess what? These are actually qualities within yourself that are being reflected back on you. Isn't that a frightening thought?

I know I really got defensive the first time I reflected on my list. "But that's not me… Right?!" As my husband (who is very grounded) gently pointed out, the bigger lesson here is that when we encounter people who we don't like or who "rub us the wrong way", we need to think about treating them with compassion because, after all, the elements we are responding to are within us as well. From this practice, we learn more self-compassion (which most of us could use a lot more of!).

There's no question that likeability is a factor that can contribute to your career prospects. Personally, I think the behaviours that both Sanders and Bhargava talk about in their books are all good practices to employ and develop, but whether they'll increase your likeability factor with everyone you meet, well, don't hold your breath. Not everyone's going to like you and not everyone's going to want to work for you. Even if other people think you're the best boss in the world, it doesn't mean everyone will.

So don't over stress about likeability. Just do the best you can and work on managing the strong parts of your leadership approach that may hold a negative (remember, every strength can be a liability). And try to build compassion and empathy for others that rub you the wrong way while doing the same for yourself. We are all works in progress.

And, finally, if you find you are generally liked by people in other parts of your world but people at work don't seem to like you no matter what you do, it may be them, not you. Find a culture that appreciates your unique style and likes you for you.

Saving Face: How Defensiveness Can Undermine Your Leadership

What gets your back up? Is it when people accuse you of being disorganized? Or suggest that you're not capable of handling a particular situation? Or perhaps when your work is criticized? We all get defensive, but have you ever wondered why you can be sitting in a meeting with a colleague and a comment about your co-presentation gets her blood boiling and bounces off you like Teflon?

Defensiveness is triggered when someone attacks the "face" we are presenting to the world. We all present a face (or often multiple faces). You want your direct reports to see you as a firm, friendly and fair boss, but you want your peers to see you as someone who's fun to hang out with; and you want your boss to see you as their right-hand and confidante. You present yourself differently to each group.

When someone starts to challenge the face you've presented, you're going to want to defend yourself. Here's an example: you want to be seen (and see yourself) as a fair boss, so when your direct report complains that it's unfair for Suzy in accounting to get first dibs on vacation time because she doesn't have much tenure, you may immediately feel the need to defend yourself.

Defensiveness comes in many forms:

Attacking the critic either through direct verbal aggression *(Why are you worrying about Suzy's vacation time when you're still way behind on your project, Jane?)* or through sarcasm *(Geez, you're right Jane. Guess I should have checked with the tenure police before approving that!)*

Distorting key information by rationalizing the situation *(Well, Suzy has only been here for a little while, but she's been working a lot of overtime and I felt that* *breaking protocol would be OK in this situation)* or by compensating for the issue *(Jane you're right. I totally forgot about that tenure piece. I'll tell you what, why don't you and the rest of the group take next Friday off as a bonus day as a way of an apology?)*

Finally, excuses as to "why" things can't be done *(I'm really sorry Jane, but at this point I can't make any changes because it's already gone to HR.)* If we change "can't" to "won't" in that sentence we can see what's really being said is "I don't want to admit I've screwed up."

Once you start down a defensive path, it can begin to spiral downwards quickly. Bosses who get defensive when challenged quickly start to shut down input and ideas. To get the best out of our people, we need to be able to handle criticisms that may cut a little close to our self-image. Here are some tips to help stop the defensive spiral:

1. **Seek to understand.** Take a breath and ask your critic questions to get a better understanding of the issues. Seek specifics and, if they're not offered, guess at the specifics to get a clear understanding of where the person is coming from. This can help reduce your initial defensiveness and give you a better view of the situation.

2. **Agree with the critic or their perception.** This approach allows you to acknowledge things that are true and also avoid any debate over who's right and who's wrong. *(Now that you mention it, it wasn't fair for me to approve Suzy's vacation without considering tenure.)*

3. **Pause and reflect.** After a particularly negative interaction where you've been defensive, take a few moments to identify what triggered your feelings. By being aware of your own hot buttons, you'll be able to avoid traps that make you defensive in future conversations.

As leaders, we face criticism on a daily basis. Think about the people with whom you become the most defensive. What parts of your "presenting self" do you defend the most? What are the typical outcomes from your defensive interactions? Now, how can you act differently in the future? Set an intention for yourself on how you want to show up next time your defensive hot button gets pressed.

Zombie Boy and Lessons in Perspective Shifting

Have you seen Rick "Zombie boy" Genest? He's a 26-year-old guy that has tattooed himself to look like a rotting corpse. In probably one of the most effective product demo campaigns of all time, DeremablendPro showcases its product by covering up Genest's tattoos. The opening screen asks: "Do you judge a book by the cover?" and after watching it and reflecting on another conversation I had this week, it got me thinking about why it's important to challenge your perspectives about both people and situations.

Most of us would agree that being open-minded and not judging people based on their appearance is the right thing to do. But perhaps more challenging but equally important is the ability to be open-minded to others' perspectives. This can be a particularly tough exercise when you find yourself strongly disagreeing with the other person, especially if the issue is emotionally-charged. We've all probably been in situations that degenerate into unproductive arguments where name-calling or ego-clashing get in the way. The aftermath caused by those interactions is often tough to get past.

If you find yourself fuming over a recent interaction with a colleague that left you feeling angry, humiliated, frustrated or just plain lousy, try this perspective-shifting technique to get a new view on the situation and possibly a new way forward with your colleague. Essentially, this is a tool for self-reflection.

1. **You're right/They're wrong.** This is probably the easiest perspective to take. But probably not the most productive one.

2. **They're right/You're wrong.** Now try stepping into the conversation from the other person's perspective. How were they coming at the

issue? What might be true about their point of view? Time for you to be brave enough to get real about your own behaviours and intentions.

3. **We're both right/We're both wrong.** What learning can you extract from the situation? What are you accountable for and what could you do differently in the future?

4. **The issue isn't as important as it seems.** After reflecting on each perspective, what remains? Was this just a hot-headed blow-up over something minor that, in the grand scheme of things, isn't important? If so, let it go. If not, what have you learned that can help you and the other person move forward?

I learned this technique which is called the pillow method many, many years ago in an intensive communications program. As a competitive individual who has a high need to win arguments, I've used it ever since to help me see the error of my overbearing ways and to help me process tough conversations that left me feeling less than good about the outcome.

Find a quiet spot, journal your thoughts and see where you end up. Bad interactions lead to bad relationships and bad work environments. If you want to put a relationship back on track, you may need to shift your perspective to move beyond the bad feelings and get clarity on how to get the relationship back on the rails.

Reverse Engineering Managing Up

At The Roundtable, we explore all kinds of interesting topics. One that always gets people engaged is the idea of "managing up". With the number one reason people quitting jobs being their relationship with their boss, it's little wonder that leaders in our programs spend time trying to figure out how to manage their leaders. But, here's the thing that I've found with this topic: it's one that's often taboo in organizations. Managers don't like to think that they need to be "managed". We talk about needing to manage our boss, but rarely do we talk about how our team needs to manage us! Well, guess what: we need to change that. How well are YOU at teaching your directs how to effectively manage YOU?

The reality of work relationships is that some are easy and some, quite frankly, suck. We're not going to get along easily with everyone. And, if you subscribe to the mantra of bringing diversity of thinking into your team, then there's a HIGH likelihood that many of the people on your team are going to drive you nuts. Just like you're driving them nuts.

True confession: I have an awesome team. They are loyal, engaged, committed, talented and, in one way or another, are very different than me – in some cases, VERY, VERY, VERY different than me. And that's good. That's why I hired them.

But does that mean it's easy for me to work with everyone on my team ALL the time? Absolutely not. Is it easy for them to work with me all the time? DEFINITELY not!

Like many of you, we've spent lots of time in our company looking at our individual "strengths" and "preferences" and all that awareness is helpful. However, in my experience, it doesn't always translate into concrete changes that improve your working relationship. Invariably, our tendency as human beings is to look at results of things like Myers Briggs, DiSC, etc. and say: "Look at how awesome my style is. Too bad everyone else is so deficient."

When someone's style is completely different than your own, you need to be explicit about what they need to do to work more effectively with you. Help them help you. The more transparent and clear you can be, the easier it is for them to do the few key things that will keep you in line and off their backs. If you don't tell them that you are a detail person and need to see facts and figures, how will they know that except through trial and error? (And countless frustrating meetings on both your parts.)

By clearly stating your expectation and what you need from your direct reports, you are helping them understand what your hot buttons are and what you need to see from them. This is going to reduce their frustration and make you happier as well.

Does this mean that you don't need to adapt your style to your direct reports? Of course not. We all know that leadership is about being adaptive to different needs; however, this is a partnership. Don't do all the heavy lifting yourself. It's OK for you to have expectations of your directs on how they can make your life easier, just as they have expectations of you.

Leadership today is about shared success and the best way to build a productive partnership with your team members is to teach them how to do it.

#PEOPLE: THE TRICKY BITS

Have you ever had the experience where, no matter how much feedback you give, no matter how much you adapt your leadership style, no matter how firm, friendly or fair you try to be, some direct reports continuously break the rules and are difficult to work with? I've learned that strong leadership is about knowing when it's time to let someone go. When I find myself working harder than my direct report to make the work situation better, I've realized that maybe this just isn't the spot for them. They're probably not intentionally being a jerk, but something about the fit just isn't working for either of us. I now try to have those "career conversations" earlier so that we can both get on with our lives.

Lessons in Recruiting From the Trenches

Skills and experience get you hired; attitude and behaviour get you fired. That's an oft-quoted managerism that speaks to the importance of, in Jim Collins' words, "getting the right people on your bus." Too often, we use gut feelings and surface first impressions (e.g. their resume, how well the person interviews, rapport) to make our hiring decisions. Spending more time upfront on your interviewing can save you lots of time and money down the line.

Before getting thrown in head first to the world of assessment, I conducted countless management interviews using the same toolkit of questions: what are your strengths, what are your weaknesses, etc. I used to spend most of the time asking people to tell me what they would do in certain situations. I made some good hires, but I also made some terrible hires. Here are five interviewing 101 lessons that I've picked up along the way. When I use them (and that's the key!), they are surprisingly effective.

Lesson #1 – Past behaviour predicts future behaviour. In a nutshell, this means ditch the "what would you do if" questions and ask: "Tell me about a time when…" This is behavioural interviewing at its most basic. By hearing the candidate tell you about a real situation (actually, a number of real situations), you get to hear how they actually dealt with something vs. their fictional version of how they would deal with something.

Lesson #2 – Dig deeper. Building on the first lesson, when listening to the past story, make sure you probe out to get specifics. Listen for the following key components:

Situation: Have they described what was going on clearly?

Task: What was the task they were doing/their role in the situation?

Action: What actions did they take?

Result: What were the outcomes? How did they feel? What did they learn?

Lesson #3 - Ask about their values. In my opinion, an alignment between a person's core values and those of the organization is crucial for long-term success. One way to find out about the person's values is to straight up ask them, but don't be surprised if you get a blank stare. If that's the case, ask them for five people they really admire and what it is about those people that they admire. Another option is to find out what they think former colleagues would say about them. From there, listen to their answers and see if you can "hear" some of the values come through. You're not looking for a direct match to your organization's culture, but someone who values teamwork heavily, may not fit well in an "eat what you kill" culture where it's every person for themselves.

Lesson #4 - Shut up. Too many interviewers spend the first 30 minutes of a 60-minute interview giving the candidate an "overview" of the role and the company. Depending on how persuasive your candidate is, all that does is give them lots of fodder to feed you the right lines. In a first interview, a brief setup and overview of the interview process (five minutes) should kick it off and save the last 15 for candidate questions.

Lesson #5 - Max out the reference requests. Ever wonder where asking for three references came from? My former boss used to get us to ask for nine. As he pointed out, it's easy to dig up three people who love you, but nine is more of a stretch. Now, it doesn't mean you have to call all nine, but if the first boss you call gives you some red flag info, you have two more bosses to go to if you want to put your concerns to rest.

Bonus Lesson #6 - Hire slowly, fire fast. Getting the right person on your bus from the get-go is probably one of the most important management activities you can do, so make sure you have the right fit. Getting comfortable and competent at interviewing is a key tool for your toolkit. But we all make mistakes. If you make one, there's no sense ripping the Band-Aid off slowly – for anyone involved. Once you've recognized the fit isn't there, it's best for your employee, and you, to move on.

Hire for Fit... What I've Learned Through a Career of Miss-Hires

You hire for skills, you fire for lack of fit. It's a lesson I was told about leadership early on in my career and continually seem to ignore. I lived through a couple of hiring missteps recently on my team. I'm sure I'm not the only leader out there who has a penchant for repeating missteps in hiring, so it got me wondering, why is it that we often ignore our gut or facts and move forward with suboptimal hires. Here are a few of my own reflections based on my twenty-five-year hiring career:

Your strength becomes your liability. One of my strengths is unwavering optimism. Whether it's related to my business (always awesome!), my clients (totally the BEST!) or my ability to navigate tough situations (who doesn't love a challenge!), being optimistic has been a huge asset to me as an entrepreneur.

As a hiring manager though, it's a bit of a curse. Instead of heeding red flags in assessments or from references, I can find a way to talk myself into things by deluding myself into believing I can make it work. What are your strengths that may actually trip you up in the hiring process?

Great talent is hard to find. Often we look to hire people when we're really stuck and need the help. Instead of continuously scanning for great talent on an ongoing basis, we find ourselves behind the Magic 8-Ball and scrambling to fill key roles. The whole interview process can last anywhere from two to six weeks, so it's no wonder that it's tough to go back to the drawing board if someone isn't "quite right" but "good enough". I know I've avoided it and "settled". Keep an active talent funnel.

Don't make it personal. Sometimes people come to you as "friends of friends". One organization I worked at actually gave people a bonus for recommending friends and colleagues. If you're a high empathy person, it may be difficult to separate business from personal, and you may tolerate mediocre or poor performance because you don't want to hurt someone's feelings. Ultimately, this is a detriment to you and the person you're tolerating. Whose feelings are you avoiding hurting?

Poor fit will kill your culture. Each time our team sheds an individual who was a poor fit, the shift in the dynamic is palpable. Where we would find ourselves "stuck" or "grinding" to get through issues and work, we would instead pick up momentum and move faster, even though we were short-staffed. In my experience, the right people can get three to four times the amount of work done than the effect a poor fit has on your team and culture. Who's slowing your team down?

Hiring the right person takes time. Don't give up if the right person isn't there the first time around. The right fit is worth the wait.

How to Spot a Talent Repellent

I don't know when I first heard the phrase "talent magnet", but it was probably sometime around the same time we started throwing around words like "employee engagement" and "high potential". In the "war for talent", we were all told that leaders who become "talent magnets" are great at attracting great talent to their teams and their organizations.

I once worked with a colleague who my then-boss referred to as a "talent repellent". It made me laugh at the time, but the reality is that our organizations are filled with people who repel talent. Here's my list of behaviours that can make some people so off-putting:

1. **Won't stop talking about their MBA.** We get it. You're smart. You got an MBA twenty years ago. But what have you done since then? If you're using phrases like "When I was in school getting my MBA…", just stop. No one really cares and you've already used that card, so move on.

2. **Always need to get the last word in.** Really smart people do this all the time. They need to show everyone how smart they are. Sometimes there's great benefit to just shutting up and letting other people feel good about their ideas rather than trying to "one-up" them with your brilliance.

3. **Being aware of "bad" behaviours and continuing to use them.** Self-awareness as a leader is usually a good thing, unless you use it as an excuse to continue behaving badly. Saying "Yes, I know it's not *what* I'm saying but *how* I'm saying it" does not give you license to continue to verbally bully people. Yes, changing behaviour is hard, but if it's impacting those around you negatively, you're the only person who can do something about it (and remember, *you're* the leader!).

4. **Perfectionism.** This is such an annoying behavior, which – in my experience – is usually rooted in insecurity. It often comes out as controlling, micromanaging behaviour and is sometimes passable with very inexperienced junior staff, but will have senior people running for the doors faster than you can say "I'd prefer the line on that Excel sheet to be three points wider."

5. **Forever being the critic.** It's one thing to debate ideas, but to be around someone who is continuously looking at the downside of the situation is emotionally draining. It's important to balance realism with optimism if you want people to be excited to work with you.

Talent repellers are pretty easy to spot in organizations. They're the ones who have a hard time retaining senior staff; usually have junior staff in perpetual states of tears; and who – although say all the right things when they get feedback – make only very minor changes to their behaviours.

So why aren't these people canned? In my experience, it goes back to their smarts. They're often very bright people who deliver results. The rest of the negative behaviour gets overlooked. It takes a pretty bold (and courageous) leader to move someone like that out of the organization. Sadly, it often seems that the short-term pain of losing these individuals outweighs the long-term gain that would come with putting someone into the team that could attract, retain and grow great talent. What a shame. Do you know a talent repellent in your organization? What qualities would you add to our list?

#PEOPLE: THE TRICKY BITS

The Dirty Little Secret About Leadership

In 2009, there was some serious hubbub over Canada's sullied reputation on addressing climate change issues at the global summit in Copenhagen. Word was that Canada could adopt a controversial move to allow oil and gas companies to get special tax breaks in order to "remain competitive" once proposed efforts to reduce greenhouse gas emissions kick in.

At the time, then Canadian Environment Minister Jim Prentice was coy in saying that he wouldn't close the door on the possibility that Canada may need to introduce a bill that offers tax breaks in order to allow the oil and gas industry to remain competitive and in line with the United States.

From the *Globe and Mail*: *"The bill would help some of these industries adapt to emissions caps and clean-energy regulations by giving them special allowances to cover their higher costs… Any U.S. industries that fall into the trade-sensitive category should be granted similar treatment in Canada."*

It's this kind of action that tarnishes Canada's global reputation as being a progressive, "green" country – a position that many Canadians identify with and want to be known for on the world stage. By making allowances to polluting companies, we're not living our collective values!

Which leads us to the dirty little secret of leadership: it's hard to cut your top performer, even if they're polluting your world.

Let's face it, oil sands (which is on environmentalists' top 10 "hate" lists due to their excessively high emissions) are a high performer for the Canadian economy on which a lot of people are making a lot of money.

In corporate speak, they're akin to that self-centered, abusive, high-performing sales executive who brings in 60% of your annual budget. If that guy is on your team and you're his boss, it's tough to actually "do the right thing" and cut bait, especially when your own personal bonus (think re-election) is going to take a hit. Letting go of individuals who don't live the values but who drive big results is much harder than firing the guy who's not living the values AND not delivering results.

And that's the dichotomy of leadership. You really want to be that authentic leader that lives the values **AND** delivers results, but ultimately, you'll be rewarded on what drives your bottom line.

Leadership takes courage. It also requires sacrifice. By letting go of that arrogant high-performing sales guy, you'll take a short-term hit on your bottom line. However, over the long-term, you'll be living your values and, as many would suggest, will be building an organization, division or team that will ultimately produce greater things than any one performer can possibly do. Isn't that what being a leader is really all about?

Right now, we have global leaders who are feeling the short-term pressure of big business: pressure to bend the rules and, as a result, sacrifice the long-term health of our planet. Short-term decisions may win the next few elections, but we need global leadership that looks at things over the long term. We need the same in our organizations.

So, what tough leadership choice are you going to make today?

Silent Witness: Why Bullies Thrive in Today's Workplace

In 2014, CBC on air personality Jian Ghomeshi was charged with a number of counts of sexual assault (he was later acquitted). As the charges came to light, other stories emerged about Ghomeshi's penchant for workplace harassment and bullying. Hearing about the charges made me sick, but what made me angry was knowing that there were numerous leaders walking the halls at CBC who knew about his abusive behaviour and did nothing about it.

We know we shouldn't tolerate jerks in the workplace, so why do we? I'm sure that the vast majority of leaders at the CBC are good people trying to do good work, like leaders in most organizations. So why didn't any of them stop Jian Ghomeshi in his arrogant, bullying tracks?

Here's my observation: Throughout history, the vocal minority has bullied the silent majority. The late comedian George Carlin once said: "Never underestimate the power of stupid people in large groups." Well, I say never, ever, ever underestimate the power of narcissistic megalomaniacs who deliver results in performance-obsessed organizations.

With more and more pressure being put on leaders to drive results – in the case of CBC leaders, there is an ongoing battle to prove the viability of public broadcasters, so of course highly-rated programs and hosts are going to carry clout – more and more leaders are making deals with the devil.

It's all interconnected: executive compensation gets tied to performance; results "at any cost" begin to trump "results the right way"; integrity gets blurry as leaders' personal needs, wants and lifestyle requirements get tied to corporate growth targets that are becoming increasingly unrealistic.

So, it's very easy to say that we shouldn't put up with jerks – Bob Sutton wrote a great book about it called *The No Asshole Rule* – but to make this stick takes courage and a deep belief that, by cutting loose your abusive star performer, the team will rise up and achieve even higher results. It can seem like a gamble and – for leaders who are trapped by their own needs and wants – may seem like too much of one. "Do I really want to fire my arrogant top sales guy when I know he brings in 80% of the revenue which drives my own comp plan? I really want to pay off my mortgage this year."

Here's the thing. Nobody said leadership was easy. It's not. **A true leader makes tough calls and sometimes has to sacrifice things that are good for themselves for things that are for the greater good of the team.**

Who are you currently enabling at your workplace that you know needs to go? What I know for sure is that the short-term pain of making tough calls on abusive, bullying employees is well worth the long-term gain you get from having a happy and productive team. I promise.

Micro Aggression at Work: Are You Unintentionally Supporting Workplace Bullying?

Pink Shirt Day – aka anti-bullying day – encourages kids across Canada to sport pink t-shirts and talk about how to be kinder to each other. In the parallel grown-up world, we introduce Bill 168 to stop workplace harassment. All good moves, but in my experience as both a parent and a working adult, once put into the spotlight, bullying has a tendency to go underground. Many people at work are being robbed of their self-confidence through a subtle form of workplace bullying which I'm going to call micro-aggressions.

In grade 7, some mean girls were giving my then 12-year-old a hard time. The issues got surfaced, kids were spoken to, tears were shed and promises were made to be kinder and more inclusive. The bullying didn't stop. It simply went underground. My daughter began dealing daily with what the school labelled "micro-aggressions", little actions that, when taken alone, seem like "no big deal" but, over time, negatively affect confidence and self-esteem. In her world, kids moved seats to sit with another group; they whispered and didn't share what was being discussed; they wouldn't invite her to lunch; and excluded her from tags on Instagram photos. It was brutal and tough to address.

In the work world, overt bullying in organizations is easy to deal with. Someone screams at you, someone hits you, someone harasses you publicly – in all these cases, you have a lot of options. What's harder – and much more insidious – are the micro-aggressions that add up over time. For example: your leader doesn't like you, so they give you a lousy performance review (nothing too horrible but just enough to affect your brand) or they badmouth you to other influential people through the guise of trying to be "helpful" (i.e.: "Oh, Ellen's great, we just need to work on her ability to drive to deadlines"). They leave you out of key meetings "by accident". They red-pen your work perpetually. They take credit for your ideas.

All of these small actions, especially when delivered by someone you know doesn't like you, can, over time, erode your self-confidence. If you're not careful, these become a self-fulfilling prophecy leading to career derailment. You start questioning your abilities and live up to the low bar set by your bullying boss.

Bullying is all about power and people who hold leadership roles can sometimes wield that power in a negative way. Usually, those around the bully and the victim know exactly what's going on ("Boy, John really doesn't like Susan" or "Don't get on Joe's bad side, he'll blacklist you!"). Many bullies in organizations have a very clear reputation. Usually they know how to get shit done so people higher up the food chain like them. Because of that, they hold power beyond their positional power. This power causes the people around the person to stand by and say nothing. They can see that a colleague is being picked on but rather than step up and say something, they keep quiet out of fear of losing their own status and/or potentially becoming the target themselves. It's the typical by-stander effect.

If you're in a situation where you're being subtly bullied by a senior leader, your best move is, frankly, to get away from that person with your reputation intact. Expand your network and build allies beyond your area. Make sure other people have first-hand experience with your work as much as you can. **Don't let your bullying boss be the only person who can offer a perspective on your performance.**

For the rest of us who see a colleague being unfairly treated, please don't be a coward. Find ways to share your concerns with others in more influential ranks who may listen. One of the things I've learned through my daughter's experience is that if bullies aren't dealt with, they start to poison the entire environment. Find someone who has more power than the bully and get their advice on how to handle the situation. Confronting the bully head on likely won't work and, if that person's a high performer, you're going to need quite a few allies who see through the behaviour to convince senior leaders there's a problem. If your company has a strong set of corporate values, be sure to use them as a foundation for voicing your concerns.

Does this feel like a political play? It probably is. The problem for many of us is that we don't like to acknowledge that organizations, by their very nature, are political. Even companies that espouse the fact that they're "not political" end up being political. Bullies are typically well-versed at playing the game, which is why they get away with what they do.

As leaders, we have an obligation to do our best to weed out this type of subversive bullying behaviour. I don't think it's easy to do, but maybe if we try to be kind and non-judgmental ourselves, maybe if we ask questions and don't take comments about other people at face value, if we dig deeper into situations to understand ALL perspectives, not just the perspective of the bully, maybe we'd get a little closer to the truth and to taking away the power from these kinds of people.

Don't be a by-stander.

Workplace Bullies:
Lessons from Hillary Clinton

Watching the second debate between Hillary Clinton and Donald J. Trump in the 2016 American Presidential election will likely go down in history as one of the most uncomfortable pieces of theatre ever aired. Since the debate aired, memes have been made, musical scores have been created and opinion pieces written. In real time, millions of people watched as one opponent used classic tactics to try and intimidate and bully the other with his physical presence, flagrant lies and body language. It was fascinating and unnerving at the same time. And, it's something most of us have to deal with at work as well. There are always some people who get extreme pleasure in bringing others down, especially in public.

You know these people. They're the ones that always seem to ask the question that you're not prepared for in a meeting. Or they throw out some crucial tidbit of information that could have been shared weeks earlier. They are described by colleagues as "sharks" or "vultures" and love the smell of blood in a boardroom. Make no mistake: this is a form of bullying. If you have someone in your company who makes a sport out of making you or others look inept, here's how to shut them down, Hillary style:

1. Never sink to their level: One of Trump's tactics was to parade out a bunch of Bill Clinton's former lovers and accusers. Since he himself had had a number of lovers during the course of his three marriages, Hillary could have thrown a few choice words his way about his personal life. Instead, she kept focused on her message of policy. As a result, she came across as the stronger and more stable presenter.

Your workplace bully may bring up past screw-ups you've made, which may make it tempting to point out his or her own shortcomings. Stay focused on your message and you will show as the bigger person and your challenger as a petty interrupter.

2. Keep focused on your audience: Trump's stalking and invading of Clinton's personal space throughout the debate was designed to distract her from her message and throw her off her game. It didn't work. She kept her focus on the people that mattered. As a result, most of the undecided attendees were firmly in the Clinton camp at the end of the debate.

Workplace bullies surf their phones or have sidebar conversations. They may stare you down or roll their eyes. Don't let that type of behaviour throw you off. Call it out if you need to or ignore it as best you can and speak to the audience in the room that matters the most.

3. Don't sink to their level, but don't be a doormat either: While Clinton sat politely as Trump took the stage, she wasn't afraid to step into his space and interrupt him when needed. Bullies don't like to be stood up to and those actions got Trump spinning further into his churlish behaviour.

Workplace bullies love hesitation. They love apologetic behaviour. Meet their interruptions and sharp questions with confident, assertive responses. Don't have an answer? No problem; say clearly and directly: "I'll get back to you on that." Made a mistake? Acknowledge it and share what your next steps to fix it will be. Don't be timid. Set your boundaries and stick to them.

4. Stay positive: I don't think Trump smiled once throughout the debate. Hillary, on the other hand, managed to keep her energy positive, despite what was – by her own admission – an incredibly uncomfortable situation.

If you know you're going into a presentation where bullying behaviour may come up, prepare for it in advance. Try some power poses to boost your confidence quotient and create some positive affirmations to set yourself up for success. These small strategies can make a big difference.

5. Surround yourself with support: Following the debate, it was interesting to see Trump and his entourage hightail it off stage as quickly as possible. Clinton, on the other hand, took her time to connect with the audience. When you've just survived being caged in with a raging lion, it's good to replenish your confidence with some well-deserved pats on the back from your supporters.

A great way to shut a workplace bully down is to get a few advocates to support you in your meeting. Talk to people ahead of time and share where you'd like their support, should things start to go sideways. Bullies often back away if they feel they're about to be outnumbered. After all, bullies are usually highly insecure and will quickly back away if they feel like they can't corral support.

And, if you see someone getting bullied in a meeting, please don't just sit and watch it happen. Intervene and show support to the person being harassed, just like we saw the moderators attempted to do for Hillary. Nobody likes a by-stander.

As a post-script, Hillary Clinton went on to lose the US election to Donald Trump in, what many have inferred, was an uneven political contest due to outside interference. Whether this proves to be true or not, there is a final lesson here if you are dealing with a workplace bully: sometimes, no matter what you do, you will never be able to win if they are being supported and backed by people with more influence than you have. In that case, it's best to let it go and move on.

My Boss is a Psychopath. What Can I Do?

One of the most fascinating things about a WordPress blog are the stats on the search phrases people use to find your blog. I'm sad to say that the phrase that gets most traffic to our blog is "my boss is a psycho" or some such variation. It's led to this post being the most read of all time.

I had lunch today with a colleague who has just landed a new job at a great place with really interesting work. Being the consummate professional that he is, he went to great pains to tell me how exciting the job is, how fortunate he feels to have one in this economy and what great potential there is for him in the role.

And then the comment came out: "The only challenge is that my boss is a bit of a psycho." Having had my own experience working for a workplace bully, I cringed as I heard the play-by-play of the behaviours that warranted this statement:

1) Condescending tone of voice: you know the kind. When you feel like you're being talked to as if you were a complete idiot even though you're a professional with 20 years of experience.

2) Eye-rolling and general "huffing and puffing" when being asked for direction. (The implied (but not verbalized) message here is: "Stop wasting my important time with your stupid little questions.")

3) Guarding of information to the point of actually restricting details necessary to allow my colleague to perform his job effectively.

4) High turnover of staff (several on stress leave) and a generally tense atmosphere with people crying in the washroom.

Which led me to my obvious question: "Why hasn't she been fired?" In my experience, you can't be a "little bit" of a psycho. If the behaviour is this consistently extreme and disrespectful, you need to be ousted.

But, for whatever reason, this manager has managed to work the system and manoeuvre through the organization, positioning herself as supposedly indispensable. Which got me thinking about what my friend could do to take matters into his own hands and get her out of the picture. This may sound completely Machiavellian, but sometimes, you have to pull out the big guns to get rid of workplace abusers. There are countless books written about this, but here is my suggestion for a four-step process to get an abusive boss fired (assuming of course that the boss in question is "fireable" and not the owner of the company!):

Step one: Begin to build relationships with key influencers at and above your boss's level. Get to know the who's who at the senior table and try and get as direct a line to them as you can; you don't want your reputation filtered to them through your boss.

Step two: Be a helpful coach to your colleagues and peers. Share strategies on how to manage the crazed boss in question. This positions you in an informal leadership role with your colleagues and aligns their allegiance more to you than your boss. This strategy can also have the bonus outcome of giving you the potential to have a shot at your boss' role once s/he is fired.

Step three: Get some visible wins under your belt with the above stakeholders (i.e. position yourself as a credible professional who gets the job done).

Step four: Build your alliances. Once wins have been established, use your new-found status as a "get it done guy/gal" to have a "Can I get your advice on this tricky situation?" chat with the senior executive (see step one) who has the most influence with the person who can fire your psycho boss.

The key to ousting a horrid manager, in my experience, is to make yourself more indispensable than them. By nurturing relationships with key senior level stakeholders, being a solid team player and over-delivering on your own projects, you may actually stand the chance of exposing and disposing of the problem boss. The "Can I ask your advice?" approach is a low-risk way of getting the message out to senior level supporters that there's a problem. Going to an influencer (vs. the person who can do the firing) is the best strategy, since they will know how to position the problem for the best impact.

Help! My Colleague is a Psycho. What Should I Do?

Several years ago, there was an article in *The Globe and Mail* that helped readers identify if they were dating a psychopath. My main take-away from that read was that the psychopath went from being completely charming and making you feel like you were the centre of his/her universe, to making you feel like less than nothing, but not because they were directly abusive.

True psychopaths have a way of manipulating and belittling you so that it slowly saps your confidence and esteem. Psychopaths are not only adept at the art of manipulation, but they see nothing wrong with their approach, as long as it's getting them what they want.

Having worked with my share of narcissistic and ego-driven people over the years, I've definitely experienced the challenges of those types of peers. So, what should you do if you find yourself working with a peer who is a bit of a pyscho? I've had this conversation with various people in similar situations at least a dozen times. I've heard all kinds of opinions, but here are the top five suggestions that I've amassed, and some thoughts on why I think they may or may not work:

1. **Use humour.** Try to diffuse the situation and let the person know that you're on to them. *The challenge as I see it with this approach is that psychopaths don't care that you're on to them. They are completely devoid of empathy and have no remorse over any of the consequences of their behaviour. I'm not sure they would get the humour and this approach might just backfire on you.*

2. **Turn the other cheek.** Steer clear of them and avoid any type of potentially negative interactions. *I like this one a bit better because, again, psychopaths aren't your garden-variety bully. They will take you down and won't*

think anything of it. Who wants to put themselves through that type of emotional torture? Better to stay away and keep your head down. Cowardly? Certainly. Effective? Only to a certain extent.

3. **Line up your allies.** Build relationships with other people at your peer, boss and senior executive levels. That way, when the psychopath starts throwing you under the bus, you have people in your corner who can offer a different perspective. *This is a good one because, at least, you'll leave question marks in others' minds and, maybe, eventually, the truth about the psycho will surface.*

4. **Line up another job, and exit gracefully.** *Sadly, I don't think true office psychopaths can be rehabilitated. Moving on may be your best option. And, before you throw a bomb out in your exit interview, consider taking the high road instead. After all, why get on a psycho's blacklist? As masters of manipulation, they'll probably find a way to make you look like the problem and them look like the hero for getting you to resign.*

People who are psychopaths are mentally ill. You cannot rationalize with a mentally ill person. They need help and medication. Sadly, highly functioning, mentally ill people are unlikely to get the help they need. In most situations I think it's best to lay low and steer clear as much as possible. If the situation gets untenable, leave.

Hopefully, you won't encounter too many psychopaths in your work life, but if you think you may be working with one, get some support for yourself. It's not you, it's them. Don't let this type of person erode your self-confidence and self-esteem.

There's no point in banging your head against a brick wall. Better to walk around it. That's my opinion; what's yours?

What Doesn't Kill You, May Kill Your Desire to Lead

When Michael Ignatieff was the leader of Canada's Liberal Party, he couldn't seem to catch a break. His popularity slid to even below that of his much-maligned predecessor, Stéphane Dion, and there was a media frenzy around his lack of leadership ability.

According to so-called "leadership experts", the true test of whether "Iggy" had the "right leadership stuff" was how he would handle this situation. Anyone who's been leading for any length of time would likely agree that adversity builds your leadership character and (hopefully) makes you stronger. After all, we typically learn more from our mistakes than when things have gone well. As history shows, Ignatieff didn't stay in his post for long and resigned. He was replaced by the younger, prettier and more media-friendly Justin Trudeau who has been managing his own set of critics and detractors.

Although most of us aren't being scrutinized to the same degree as your average politician, there does seem to be a hyper amount of criticism thrown at the average boss these days. On behalf of all managers out there **who are trying their best**, this post is aimed at you non-managers who seem to think that it is helpful to sling extra mud at a leader who is struggling.

The saying goes: "If you can't take the heat, stay out of the kitchen." I don't think that anyone would argue with the fact that today's "kitchen" for leaders is pretty damn hot. The workplace is far more challenging than it was 20 years ago and, on top of that, today's managers have markedly LESS time to lead and manage their teams. Most are drowning in their own tactical deliverables. But you may want to think twice before you drive your leader out of the kitchen.

Most people I talk to want to work for a manager who is personally supportive of them. This skill, my friends, is called **EMPATHY**, and studies have shown that leaders with higher empathy scores get more out of their teams. Period.

But here's the thing: if you work for a people-oriented boss, chances are they also take the verbal hits a little bit harder than most. And, in my observation, these are also the ones that start to question whether they could be just as effective being an "individual contributor/coach" vs. remaining in a formal management role.

This leaves the low empathy, thick-skinned leaders at the table. Is this really what we want or need in our organizations, more ego-driven, bottom-line pushing, grind-down-the-team to produce results types? Think about that for a minute.

Maybe we need to think about the type of leadership we're encouraging by how supportive we are of people who are trying their best. After all, you probably don't go into work every day trying to screw up, and I don't believe that your boss does either. Perhaps it's time to show a little empathy to the leaders from whom you are looking to get a little empathy.

DELIVER RESULTS

Section 4

#GETSHITDONE BUT DON'T BURN OUT

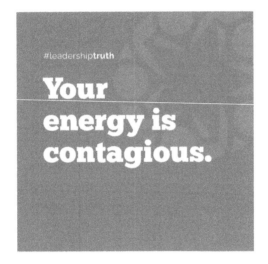

My dad was one of those people who, when he was happy, the whole world was happy and when he was angry, the energy he brought in would have you walking on eggshells. If you are a highly charismatic or high energy leader, please don't underestimate your ability to affect the energy of your team for the positive or the negative. Bad moods and negative energy are contagious. Hey, leadership can suck sometimes. When you feel yourself spiraling into negativity (I mean there's only so many losing quarters or bad results anyone can take!), make a conscious effort to bring in positive energy. One of my favourite techniques is to start off meetings with a shout out to positive things that have happened during the week. It immediately shifts the dynamic. Give it a try.

Balancing Multiple Priorities (aka How to Stay Sane)

Do you have that feeling that you're drowning in a relentless list of to-do items? Are you wondering how the heck it's "suddenly" the end of [insert week/month/year here]!!! Busy is the latest affliction causing many leaders to have sleepless nights, miss episodes of *Game of Thrones* and feverishly check their smartphones while "relaxing" on vacation. How much is too much? And what can leaders in the mid ranks do to regain control?

We posed these and other questions at one of our PowerRoundtable events to an illustrious panel of task-juggling leaders including Steve Miles (then COO International, Harlequin); Jody Steinhauer (Chief Visionary Officer, bargains group); and Cheryl Fullerton (then VP Total Rewards and Performance Management, Maple Leaf Foods). Here's what they had to say:

Time hacks

- Go ugly early. Figure out the thing you're least looking forward to in your day and do that first.

- Take the first five minutes of your day to create a to-do list and update it at the end of each day.

- Only keep three things on your to-do list to allow space for other items that will invariably pop up.

- Colour code your emails for key people based on whether you are in the "To" field or in the "Cc" field. This will help you address which ones to deal with first, and even how they need to be dealt with.

- Look to fill "wait periods" (e.g. after pushing an elevator button and waiting for it to arrive) with quick tasks and get small items off your plate rather than having them eat into your fun/personal time.

Managing your boss

- Review your to-do lists with your boss on a regular basis. Make sure your priorities are still their priorities.
- Don't just blindly take work from a superior. Confirm how new activities advance the big agenda items. If they don't, ask where they fit on the priority list.
- Don't assume your boss understands the amount of work that may be required. Be sure to clarify if items are "need to know" or "nice to know" before embarking on a ton of work. Ask your boss a question like: "What would you (boss) do differently if you had that info?" If their answer is nothing, then it's probably not the right thing to work on.

Self-care

- Determine what you're in control of and what is beyond your area of responsibility. Don't confuse accountability with responsibility.
- Set boundaries with technology. It's important to have downtime.
- You must put yourself first. Make self-care a value. Get enough sleep. Find the time to do what you love. Learn when you are most productive and use that time to your advantage.

Build team capacity

- Make sure you're delegating appropriately. Value your own time and make sure you're not spending it on tasks that are below your level of responsibility/seniority.
- Determine where people are and where they need to be. Think of the skill/will matrix. (Do they have the skill but not the will? Or do they have the will but not the skill? Both? Or neither?) Depending

on the mix of your team you may need to look at training, incentives or other methods to help them take on more.

- Be accountable and hold others accountable. Don't step in to "pick up the pieces". Have the tough conversations needed to improve performance.

Challenge the status quo

- It's always a good idea to take a step back and question the value of something (don't do it just because it's always been done). Meetings are a good example of this, unless the meeting is to share information people need, or to make a decision, you shouldn't have one.

From my perspective, we are in an accelerated world where our to-do lists will always be never ending. It is very easy to get caught up in what we "should" do versus what me "must" do. Since becoming a business owner, my focus for myself and my team has been to continually ask ourselves three questions: how is what I'm doing right now making us money, saving us money or helping our clients? If the answer is "it's not", then it becomes easier to decide what to stop doing. Because of the speed of change, it's important to keep asking these questions on a regular basis. What may have been a priority last month may be today's old news.

Aristotle and the Art of the Habit

Are you a believer in New Year's Resolutions? Do you start strong each year and fade by the end of January? A few years ago, I was lucky enough to be part of a dynamic leadership project for next gen leaders that went far beyond traditional classroom training. It's been a great learning experience for me, particularly around how you can create rituals to actually get those "resolutions" to stick. One of the presenters used a quote from Aristotle that I'm inspired to share:

"We are what we repeatedly do. Excellence, then, is not an act, but a habit."

Malcolm Gladwell and Geoff Colvin both wrote bestselling books *(Outliers* and *Talent is Overrated*, respectively) based on the idea that hours of practice trumps talent. While certainly the idea of practice making perfect isn't new, it's the discipline to actually **do** the practice that's the killer for most of us, hence all those broken New Year's Eve resolutions.

According to research, **95% of what we do is automatic**.

Think about that for a minute. That means **only 5% of what we do is driven by conscious choice**. So, if we want to make new habits stick, we need to build positive and highly specific rituals (behaviours) that become automatic overtime (like brushing your teeth every morning).

The key to creating a new ritual that will eventually become a habit is to get very, very specific. Think about when you are going to do this new habit, where, with who, how often and why it's important to you in the first place. And don't try to take on too much. If you're someone who finds it hard to hold yourself accountable, then enlist others to help you.

Be sure to focus on starting something new vs. trying to "stop" something. You can apply the practice of creating rituals to your personal or professional life. Apply it to goals you want to attain or to behaviours you want to instill, and, before you know it, you may find that your ritual of leaving work at 5 p.m. on Monday, Wednesday and Friday has become an automatic habit. Nice!

The key difference between really successful people and others is their ability to be disciplined around their important rituals in the domains of physical, mental, spiritual, and emotional health. You can do it. Just figure out the support you need to make it happen.

Lessons from the World Cup of Soccer: How to Push an Agenda

As the offspring of a rugby football player, I have to confess that following soccer was not something that was actively encouraged in my house, but the Canadian soccer teams' failure to qualify for the 2018 FIFA World Cup in Russia caught my attention.

There was much chatter about why Canada failed and what we, as a country, need to do to make our mark on the "world's" game. As the Canadian Soccer Association plots to get soccer on the national sports funding agenda, there are some great takeaways for any leader trying to get their agenda heard.

Listening to some Canadian soccer experts talk about why Canada isn't a dominant player on the international soccer stage, the hurdles seem to boil down to:

- **Inadequate coaching.** Our coaches just aren't on top of the latest techniques.
- **Insufficient practicing.** The feeder system for soccer emphasizes playing games, not practicing technique. To take your play to another level, you need to move to Europe.
- **Underfunding.** Canada has a history of underfunding sport in comparison to other countries. Soccer is no different.
- **Lack of motivation/passion to embrace the World Cup objective.** Canadians already have a national game tied closely to the country's identity, and a cup named Stanley. Who needs a new one?

So, spinning the hurdles into "must-haves", here's a list of things that the Canadian Soccer Association – and YOU – need to put in place to get to the table:

- **The right talent (leadership).** It's easier to sell an idea when you can prove you have the talent to make it happen. You may need to hire new talent, mentor others or upgrade the skills on your existing team.

- **Know what skills and behaviours will make your team successful.** Being clear on who you need and what they will need to do is probably the most crucial ingredient for any team. After that, weaving the building and practicing of these skills into an ongoing part of the team's activities will help you regularly raise the bar. In the world of "we need this yesterday", building in solid performance improvement programs is easy to overlook. Sink or swim is too often the on-the-job training program. (Hands up everyone who has a great orientation program not just for new hires but for people who are promoted from within.)

- **Ask for money AND time.** Launching new initiatives on a shoestring budget is often a recipe for disaster. Without adequate funding and support, your initiative will slowly derail. On top of that, like Canada's goal to "Own the Podium" in 2010, achieving lofty goals takes time. If you don't fight for reasonable timelines, along with the funding, you'll find yourself behind the eight ball before you've even begun.

- **Assess the will to support your idea.** This is perhaps the most important component of all. Do you have a critical mass within your organization that believes in your idea and support you? If people don't care/don't understand/don't see the need for your new initiative, you may need to build up your base of support before proceeding. And for this to occur, timing is everything.

For Canadian fans who would love to see their country on soccer's world stage, the tides may be shifting. Immigration has brought in thousands of ardent soccer fans who may provide some of the momentum needed to bring forward the national soccer federation's agenda. We probably won't be seeing Canada in a FIFA World Cup anytime soon, but with the right elements in place and a healthy dose of patience and perseverance, who knows? The World Cup may just find its way onto Canadian soil sometime before 2030.

The Value of the Third Opinion: How to Find a Mentor

Coaches, mentors and peer groups have been incredibly helpful to me at various stages of my career and, in my opinion, continue to be some of the most misunderstood and underutilized tools for many leaders. The value of mentors and how to find and work with them is particularly misunderstood.

Mentors can bring value in many different areas. I'm going to focus here on finding a mentor who will help you with your **LEADERSHIP SKILLS.**

In my experience, a leadership mentor can help you in the following ways:

- Navigate new levels of decision-making
- Offer a different perspective/vantage point on politics and priorities
- Expand your thinking about your career options
- Provide a different viewpoint
- Access technical skills and techniques in "real time"
- Increase both your interpersonal and technical leadership tools.

The first important thing to know about finding a leadership mentor is that you need to find someone who's been at least two or three levels higher than where you currently are, with bigger scope and years of hands-on leadership experience. Here are some basic steps to finding and working with a leadership mentor:

Know your goals. Why do you want to work with a mentor? What do you want to gain from the experience? The mentor needs to be a combination of knowledge expert and coach, so knowing what it is that you want to learn is key.

Ask for recommendations. Once you have a clear picture in your mind of the type of support you need, ask your network for suggestions. Look for executives who like to "help", not ones who are mostly interested in self-promotion.

Start small. Once you've identified the person you'd like to work with, approach them to see if they'd be willing to work with you for a 6-month period (aim for once-a-month meetings). Start small with one specific (tactical) request to see if the relationship has potential.

Be prepared. To make the meetings work for you and for your mentor, get focused before each one. Know what you have accomplished and what you want to discuss moving forward.

Recognize when it's time to move on. Once your main objectives are accomplished, it's time to move on (or else you'll find yourself having great "coffee talks" and not much more). By setting out a clear 6-month cycle, you can talk about renewing for another term if you both feel there's still work to be done or shift to a looser relationship if the main issues have been addressed.

One final piece of advice: many of the senior executives I work with seem to get scared if you throw the word "mentor" at them. For many, it's too big a responsibility and, for others, it sounds like something that's never going to end. "It's impossible to get rid of mentees," a few have grumbled to me. You may, therefore, need to be more "stealth-like".

Also, think about having multiple mentors, both internally and externally. In my experience, one size doesn't fit all and it's important to have a few people on your "team" to help you be successful. Again, it's all about being clear on where you need the support and what role they can play.

And remember, mentoring is a very self-directed form of learning. As the mentee, you'll get as much or as little out of the experience as you put into it.

Are You a Frog Being Boiled Alive?

The story goes that if you place a frog in a pot of boiling water, it will immediately leap out to safety. If, however, you put the frog in a pot of water at room temperature and slowly increase the heat, the frog will stay put even as the water reaches its boiling point – and you'll be enjoying frog legs for dinner.

The analogy of the boiled frog is a metaphor for some of the craziness we're inflicting on ourselves in workplaces today. We're creating cultures where individuals are losing sight of what's normal and what's completely unhealthy. When intern Moritz Erhardt was found dead in his London flat in 2013 after working three days straight, he had most certainly been boiled to death by Merrill Lynch's warped company culture.

Here is our quick checklist to help you recognize if you're a frog that is being boiled alive:

- You have a goal to leave the office early at least three times a week to have supper with your kids… With "early" being 7 p.m.
- You get up on vacation to respond to work emails in the morning so that you can "enjoy" the rest of your day with your family.
- When at [insert fun location here], you believe that checking messages without responding doesn't count as work.
- You have missed your child's [fill in the blank] on more than one occasion because you "had" to work late.
- Your boss has his assistant walk around at 5 p.m. to take pictures of who is still at their desks.
- You fully believe that if you don't log XXX hours per week, you will lose your chance for promotion (sadly, you may be right).

- You're tired of hearing yourself say "exhausting" or "hectic" when your family asks how your day was.
- You leave the office at 5 p.m. but flip your laptop on after everyone's in bed and work until 1 a.m. on a consistent basis, four days a week.
- You regularly blow off going to the gym, seeing friends, doing leisure activities because you "have" to work late.
- People in your office who leave before [fill in the blank] are seen as slackers.
- You "can't" take a 2-week vacation.
- You "can't" completely unplug when you're on vacation.
- You "can't" not check in with the office at least once a day when you're on vacation.
- You regularly work through your lunch hour.

For the record, if you answered "yes" to more than one of these questions, and thought to yourself "doesn't everyone?", congratulations, you are a frog that is being boiled alive. This type of over-commitment to work in sacrifice of everything else is NOT NORMAL or healthy. But over the last two decades we have normalized it, and this is something we really do need to change.

Here's what I know for sure: work culture is really challenging to change, **but it can change**. The only way it will change is if ambitious leaders like you and I step up and make it happen. We are all in great positions, and, frankly, have a responsibility to influence some of the changes that need to be made. To begin, start with yourself. What changes are you going to make to turn down the heat in your own teams? What kind of ripple effect will that create within your organizations? My friend Dr. David Posen wrote a book called *Is Your Work Killing You?* It certainly did kill Moritz Erhardt, but it doesn't have to kill anyone else. Don't you agree?

Own the Podium: When Stretch Targets Go Bad

After the Canadian Olympic team fell short at the 2014 Sochi Olympics, there was lots of handwringing and apologizing going on from the Own the Podium committee, athletes and the media at large. Were the targets too high? Was the Own the Podium goal too ambitious, too arrogant? Was the pressure on the athletes too much? There's a lesson here for all leaders in the importance of setting targets that motivate.

After spending years running businesses and sales teams, I am of the firm view that the ability to achieve a target is a blend of a number of factors, including:

- The environment (market/economy, etc.)
- The skills of the members of your team
- Your competitors' skills
- Your past track record (how are you trending)
- Your team's belief (and I mean hard core, to the bones belief) that they can achieve the goal that's been set out for them

In my experience, if you set a goal purely based on the external factors (e.g. our market's on fire, we should be able to grow 50% this year) and don't factor in other elements (e.g. your top performer is leaving and your next top performer will be going on maternity leave mid-year, plus your competitor just launched a hot new product that makes yours look obsolete), you may be in for a nasty surprise by the end of the first quarter when you see yourself sliding behind your targets.

This is where the team-belief factor really starts to kick in. Once a team feels that the target is sliding out of reach (along with their bonus), the motivation begins to slide and, in some cases, desperation starts to kick in. In my experience, that's a tough situation to get back on track from.

Own the Podium's goal was to be number one in the rankings for medals won on Canada's home turf. Was this a realistic goal given our standing coming out of Turin? Sure, we pumped millions of dollars into the program, but wasn't the Canadian sports effort chronically underfunded compared to American sports to begin with? Is four years a realistic timeframe for our athletes to catch up?

Furthermore, many of the mistakes that have cost our athletes their podium moment seem to have happened because they were going all out to get the medal and not let down the Own the Podium program or the Canadian people. Did the pressure to show that the program was a success push them to take risks they wouldn't have taken? Were they driven by desire to win or desperation not to lose? That's a huge psychological difference between the two.

In my experience, when the target is a stretch but a reasonable one, you actually increase the odds of knocking the lights out of it. One has to wonder whether the outcome would have been different if the Canadian team had put their focus on beating their Turin results, instead of owning the podium. From the look on a lot of faces, many of these athletes were robbed of the joy they should have been feeling. Snowboarder Jennifer Heil looked completely despondent after winning a silver medal, and there is something completely wrong with that.

As leaders, we need to find the right message and stretch target that pushes team performance to a new level but that doesn't encourage behaviours that may derail and demotivate. Not an easy task, but one that, when done well, can lead to amazing results.

David Packard and the Danger of Indigestion

There has never been a business process, program or plan that I couldn't see a way to improve, do differently or innovate. New ideas energize me… and drive many of the people who work for me crazy. Several years ago, my former boss and mentor, Don McQuaig, dropped a quote on my desk that said:

"More organizations die of indigestion than starvation."

The quote comes from David Packard, who, with Bill Hewlett, founded HP on $500 and a vision.

If you're at all like me and get energized and excited about new ideas, the dangerous blind spot may be that you're putting yourself (and your team) on a path to burnout. When you get your "juice" from creating or innovating, you may end up biting off more than you can chew and creating an environment where your team is doing the same.

What's helped me has been to push myself to continually revisit my priorities and use outside sounding boards (team members, coaches, mentors) to challenge my assumption on what we "absolutely have to do".

It's amazing how much you can actually cull a to-do list when you're given a rigid requirement to only focus on the top 1/2/3 things that will make the biggest impact. So, what are you going to stop doing today?

Work Hard, Work Harder: How We're Screwing up the Pursuit of Happiness

Once upon a time, in a work galaxy far, far away, there was a mantra that companies used. It went like this: work hard, play hard. Over the past decade (or possibly more), the mantra has changed to work hard, work harder, as companies move their focus from why they do what they do, to a single-minded drive to make money and increase shareholder value. Sure, there are a few bright sparks on the horizon. A handful of companies are bringing back the drive for purpose – Zappos, G Adventures, and Whole Foods, to name a few – but they are overwhelmingly few and far between. In my observation, this quest for the almighty dollar is wreaking a boatload of misery into our work lives as well as on our home lives.

During the summer of 2015, I was consumed with money conversations about our business. We were growing quickly and that required investment. As anyone who knows anything about the business growth curve will attest, when you inject capital into your business, there's a period where the costs are outweighing the future potential earnings. Layer in big investments such as new office space and new talent and it's easy to find yourself in a cash flow crunch that was getting me up at 3 a.m. thinking about payroll and how I was going to cover costs.

And that's when the downward spiral happened. The more I focussed on making money to cover bills, the more I got anxious about bringing in new business. The more anxious I was about bringing in business, the more I took my focus away from why I started my business in the first place. I began to lose my "why". Work was no longer fun. I was grinding. I started having meetings talking about how to make more money. I spent hours looking at costs to cut. I became more and more miserable.

During that time, I watched a documentary on Netflix called *Happy*. The filmmakers went on a search to find out what makes us happy. And guess what: it's not the pursuit of material goods. Once you have your basic needs met – a roof over your head, food on your plate, clothes on your back, some entertainment, there is virtually no difference in happiness levels between someone who earns $50,000 a year and someone who earns $50 million a year. Money really doesn't buy happiness. And the pursuit of money actually makes us *unhappy*. Think about that for a minute.

The pursuit of money actually makes us *unhappy*.

I detest being unhappy at work. What brings me joy is when I know I've helped a leader navigate their career a little better, or when I know I'm making a difference to a team, or when one of my colleagues hits one out of the park.

If you're feeling like you're caught in a never-ending numbers grind at work, try changing the focus. Here are a few very simple ways I do this at The Roundtable:

- I open our weekly team meetings asking people to share something great that happened to them the week before – personal or work related. Whatever makes them feel good.
- We celebrate progress, even when we're behind on budget. We look at what we've accomplished.
- We take time to appreciate each other's contributions by sharing peer feedback.
- I make a list of five of our members that I haven't spoken to in a while and reach out to see how they're doing and share a laugh.
- I read an inspiring book, watch a TED Talk or write a blog post that I think might help others.

As many of you face continued pressure to hit your numbers, try and press pause and reground yourself in your personal "why" of your own work. Think about how you can bring more happiness and balance into your life by taking the emphasis off money and material objects and putting it onto the things that ultimately matter most: love, relationships and community.

Build Your Coping Muscles: Inhale, Exhale

By: Janey Piroli

When I look at today's leadership landscape, I am increasingly concerned by the struggle to cope. The statistics paint an alarming picture. Not only are we experiencing higher levels of workplace dissatisfaction, but the rates of mental health issues and leaves are on the rise. Many leaders, including those who have a difficult time asking for help, are experiencing burnout. They push themselves so hard that, over time, they exceed their mental and emotional limits.

As leaders, we all have the responsibility to ensure that we are taking care of ourselves effectively, not just physically, but mentally and emotionally as well. There are lots of different ways in which we can develop and strengthen our inner capacity to cope. Mindfulness is one tool that can help us get there, and one which I have personally seen to be very beneficial.

My Journey

I turned to the practice of mindfulness several years back when I was having a difficult time coping with various things in my life and my work. It started with the simple act of "conscious breathing". So simple and effective, yet I didn't really understand it back then.

Over time, I started attending regular yoga classes and eventually learned what it meant to "connect with the breath". After a long day, I found solace on this rectangular mat by going inward and focusing my mind and my attention on my breath. With each inhale and each long, deep exhale, I was able to release and let go. I let go of my thoughts, I let go of my day, I became fully in the moment. By the time I left the studio, I felt relaxed, centred and whole. I soon made the connection that this was a "practice" that could be taken off of the mat and applied to everyday life.

I also learned that we all have the ability to cultivate an inner capacity to deal with difficulties in challenging times. We often look to improve a situation by shifting things that are happening outside of us. Real and lasting change, however, comes from the shift that happens within us.

The Misconception of Mindfulness

For many years, there has been confusion over the difference between meditation and mindfulness. Leaders wonder whether they will be required to sit on a cushion in lotus position for an extended period of time in order to reap the benefits of mindfulness. Simply put, meditation is a dedicated practice where one sits quietly for a period of time and focuses one's attention inward with the intention of stilling the mind. Mindfulness is about paying attention to thoughts and emotions as they arise in the present moment. It's not necessary to meditate in order to be mindful (although it helps).

One mindful breath can focus your attention and bring you back to the present moment. For those like me who may need to know why this is, the breath activates your parasympathetic nervous system and has the effect of calming you in the moment. It also has the benefit of interrupting subconscious thought streams which often lead us to react in negative ways, instead of responding with clear, focused intention.

Where to Start

I am often asked about a place to start to explore the personal benefits of mindfulness. My recommendation is to start with one mindful breath a day. Take this mindful breath whenever you begin to feel stressed, anxious or overwhelmed, or anytime you require a significant amount of mental focus and clarity. I find that it really helps me just before important meetings. As a personal reminder, I use the touch of the door handle as a cue to take a slow, deep, mindful breath before entering the room.

Inhale, exhale. Give it a try!

Thanks for Reading.
Thanks for Leading.

I hope this little volume of observations and stories about leadership has inspired you, challenged your thinking, given you something to add to your toolkit and made you chuckle.

Leadership is a journey. Every day I uncover another layer of myself and deepen my understanding into how my behaviours are shaping the work that I do. Sometimes I like the progress that I've made and sometimes I am humbled with how far I still have to go. I've learned that progress, not perfection, is the mantra we all need to embrace when it comes to developing our leadership capability.

Leadership is a wonderful opportunity to impact the lives of the people that work with us on a daily basis. As leaders, we don't have to wait until we're retired to "give back". We are in a position to give back and pay it forward every single day. What an amazing privilege that is!

I hope you continue to learn about yourself as a leader so that you can not only bring the best of yourself to others, but to you as well.

Life is filled with challenges, and leadership, by its very nature, can be lonely and isolating. In my experience, it doesn't have to be. As leaders, our hopes and fears are surprisingly similar – no matter where we work or who we work with. There is power in connecting with other leaders and exchanging ideas and strategies. When we are vulnerable and transparent, we open ourselves up to growth and find out we're all more similar than we think.

Leadership over the next two decades is going to look decidedly different. We are now in the Age of Collaboration which is forcing a re-evaluation of what great leadership actually looks like. Today's leaders will need to be adept at managing and leading in an increasingly complex and ambiguous world. Those who cultivate curiosity will strengthen their ability to be agile and adaptive and will come out ahead. Self-insight will be your greatest career advantage.

Keep growing, keep learning, keep reflecting and keep pushing yourself outside of your comfort zone. The world needs great leaders. The world needs YOU.

Happy leading!

Beef Up Your Bookshelf!

Throughout this book, I've referenced a ton of great books to read or authors and thought leaders who've provided inspiration. Here they are in one convenient shopping list.

Books I love that are referenced in the book:

First Break All the Rules, by Curt Coffman and Marcus Buckingham

Is Your Work Killing You?, by Dr. David Posen

Outliers, by Malcolm Gladwell

Soar With Your Strengths, by Donald O. Clifton

The Doom Loop, by Charles C. Jett

The No Asshole Rule, by Bob Sutton

The One Minute Manager, by Ken Blanchard

Talent is Overrated, by Geoff Colville

Tipping the Iceberg, by Tim Cork

What Got You Here Won't Get You There, by Marshall Goldsmith

I also love these books and would highly recommend picking them up to build on the themes explored:

Change Your Questions Change Your Life, by Marilee Adams

Crucial Conversations, by Al Switzler, Joseph Grenny, and Ron McMillan

Daring Greatly, by Brene Brown

Death by Meetings, by Patrick Lencioni

Fascinate, by Sally Hoggshead

Fierce Leadership, by Susan Scott

Start with Why, by Simon Sinek

The Dip, by Seth Godin

The First 90 Days, by Michael Watkins

The Five Dysfunctions of a Team, by Patrick Lencioni

The Gifts of Imperfection, by Brene Brown

BULLETPROOF YOUR LEADERSHIP CAREER

If our chapter *5 Dumb Things That Smart People Do to Derail Their Careers* piqued your interest (or sent you into a cold sweat) and you'd like to learn what steps you can take now to bulletproof your career trajectory (whatever that looks like to you), we can help!

Visit our book website (www.leadershiptruthsbook.com) and sign up for our FREE (yes you read that right), online series on five key things you can do to keep your career on track. In it, you'll learn:

- The number one thing that gets talked about in talent reviews
- Why changing behaviour is so difficult
- Three things you can do TODAY to bulletproof your future potential
- How to set up a network of support

Hope to see you there!

And for more timely leadership truths, tidbits and resources visit our website (www.goroundtable.com) and subscribe to the Roundtable RECAP, our monthly newsletter bringing you the best blogs, articles and tools to help you on your leadership journey.

ACKNOWLEDGEMENTS

For all of you leaders out there who, like me, have the fabulous ability to oversimplify and underestimate how long things will actually take, welcome to my world.

When we started talking about doing a book for our 10th anniversary, I thought it would be "simple". Just pull a bunch of the blog posts together and voila, book done. Not so much. If I had been left to my own devices to pull this thing together, you would have been waiting until our bicentennial to get a copy. So to Kim Blackwell who sifted through ten years of blog posts to pull out things that could work together, thank you for your help and support. It was invaluable. To Shannon Nedza who created the look and feel of the book and Julie Melaschenko who styles our #leadershiptruth series, it's great having both of your passion for purple perfection on the team. And to Shelby Gobbo, who has spent hours liaising with our publishing partner, proofreading and editing this volume and stick handling this project to the finish line, words of thanks just don't seem like enough! It never would have happened without your support. Kim, Shannon, Julie, and Shelby are the ones that made this thing happen.

Of course, the contents of this book simply wouldn't have been possible without all the leaders and thought leaders who've inspired me on my own leadership journey. I've learned about the good, the bad and the ugly from so many people I've had the chance to work with over the years. I'll leave out the bad and the ugly but, for the good, I will always be grateful for Jim Orban (who gave me my first job and demonstrated kind and professional leadership), Diana Carter (who trusted me and let me try and fail multiple times), the amazing women I had the opportunity to learn from at the Big

Sisters Association (Julie Evans, Francine Girard, Diana Dowthwaite, and Linda Hancock in particular) and most of all, to my late mentor Don McQuaig who role-modelled with kindness and grace how to help people work with their strengths. From Don I learned the magic that happens when you don't try and fit a proverbial square peg in a round hole.

Beyond the leaders I've worked for, we learn about ourselves as leaders from the people who work with us. I have had some fabulous colleagues over the years that have each pushed me and challenged me and helped me to grow. I feel lucky that I'm still in touch to this day with so many people that I worked with. I didn't always get it right and I know there were many days where I wasn't at my best, but to those of you who were brave enough to share feedback with me in the early years – thank you so much. I listened and I learned.

To my colleagues at The Roundtable past and present, thank you all for believing in me and for helping me continue to grow as a leader. I'm in awe of your commitment to our cause on a daily basis and am so proud of all the incredible work that you're doing.

To our Roundtable members – wow! This is a tribe of leaders who truly give a shit. I am so grateful to all of you. Thank you for sharing your stories and experiences and helping us shape our community. Together, we are learning and leading and making a difference.

Finally, to my family – my husband D'Arcy and my daughter Nia – thanks for putting up with my bossy behaviours at home. I've learned recently that the way you do anything is the way you do everything. I realize that's not always a good thing and I promise you both, I'm working on it.

ABOUT THE AUTHOR

Glain Roberts-McCabe is the founder and President of The Roundtable, a company where leaders cultivate their leadership, together.

The Roundtable is best known for their peer coaching and mentoring systems that help organizations break down silos, increase collaboration and accelerate business all while building leadership capability.

The oldest of four children (the others are all boys), Glain was born in the UK and moved to Canada when her father got a job coaching the Canadian rugby team. You might say coaching and mentoring is in her blood.

After a misguided career false start in illustration, Glain spent the majority of her twenties and thirties living the GenX career life, moving through a variety of senior leadership roles in the not-for-profit, public and private sectors. She has led across a variety of functions including public relations, marketing, membership, training, sales and spent close to a decade as a General Manager in two mid-sized businesses. Along the way, she's won a few awards, stepped on a few toes and mastered the art of the apology.

A self-professed leadership junkie, Glain has read over 1,000 leadership books, written articles for publications like *The Globe and Mail* and *Canadian Manager Magazine* and spoken to audiences around the globe. In 2014, The Roundtable was awarded a Gold Award by the Canadian Awards for Training Excellence for their peer coaching and mentoring program and in 2016 they were named Best External Consulting Advisory at the Canadian HR Awards. Both experiences were kind of like winning an Oscar but without having to wear sequins.

Glain believes that leadership is a privilege. Her personal mission is to inspire leaders to connect to their bigger purpose and passion so that work can be more fun and life can be more fulfilling.

Learn more about The Roundtable by visiting www.goroundtable.com.